P9-DUZ-879

PUGIN'S GOTHIC ORNAMENT

The Classic Sourcebook of Decorative Motifs

WITH 100 PLATES

by AUGUSTUS CHARLES PUGIN

DOVER PUBLICATIONS, INC.
New York

Published in Canada by General Publishing Company, Ltd.,
30 Lesmill Road, Don Mills, Toronto, Ontario.
Published in the United Kingdom by Constable and Company, Ltd.,
10 Orange Street, London WC2H 7EG.

This Dover edition, first published in 1987, is a republication of 100 plates originally issued by "Aug[s] Pugin, 105 Great Russell S[t]," London, between 1828 and 1831, and first published in book form as *Gothic Ornaments Selected From Various Buildings in England and France* by Preistley and Weale, London, in 1831. Plate 82, originally issued in both black-and-white and color, is here reproduced in black-and-white only. A new Publisher's Note and captions based on the originals have been prepared specially for the Dover edition.

DOVER *Pictorial Archive* SERIES

Manufactured in the United States of America
Dover Publications, Inc.
31 East 2nd Street
Mineola, N.Y. 11501

Library of Congress Cataloging-in-Publication Data

Pugin, Augustus, 1762–1832.
Pugin's gothic ornament.

Reprint. Originally published: London : Pugin, 1828–31.
1. Decoration and ornament, Gothic—Themes, motives.
I. Title. II. Title: Gothic ornament.
NK1295.P84 1987 745.4'42 87-20168
ISBN 0-486-25500-X (pbk.)

PUBLISHER'S NOTE

The life of Augustus Charles Pugin is framed by two literary events of major importance to Romanticism and the Gothic Revival. He was born in Normandy in 1762, the year in which the appearance of Macpherson's "Ossian" poems gave tremendous impetus to the Romantic Movement; he died in London in 1832, a year after the publication of Victor Hugo's *Notre-Dame de Paris,* possibly the greatest popular work sanctioning the Gothic Revival.

Pugin came to England before May 1792, when he registered as a student of painting at the Royal Academy. Some sources hold that he had left France to escape the consequences of a duel in which he had been involved; others that he feared the violence of the Revolution. Pugin soon found employment in the architectural office of John Nash (1752–1835), who had recently resumed his career in London. The association lasted 17 years and provided Pugin with some stability in a life that was a difficult one financially, attributable, in part, to prejudice against émigrés. Few of his architectural commissions are known; it was as an artist and draftsman that he made his career.

Early attempts at independent publishing failed, as did the issue of individual prints. A turn in fortune began with Pugin's work for Rudolph Ackermann (1764–1834), publisher of the monthly *Repository of Arts,* which was noted for the quality of its lithographs. Pugin was swift to demonstrate the excellence of his topological and architectural illustrations, some of which were published in separate collections. For the *Repository,* he collaborated with Rowlandson on the *Microcosm of London* (1808–10). There followed works on Westminster Abbey, Cambridge, Oxford and various public schools. Pugin also made trips abroad, primarily to France, with students from Nash's office, who served as draftsmen. Three of the most important, Benjamin Ferrey (1810–1880), Thomas Talbot Bury (1811–1877) and Joseph Nash (1809–1878), drew many of the plates in the present work and later took their own places in the English architectural establishment.

Of Pugin's works, those on the Gothic style were his most successful and enduring. His son Augustus Welby Northmore Pugin (1812–1852) accompanied him on his trips abroad and completed work on *Examples of Gothic Architecture.* Pugin *fils* became himself a renowned architect and exponent of the Gothic Revival, collaborating with Sir Charles Barry on detailing in the Houses of Parliament in Westminster.

In the British Isles, the Gothic Revival had begun early in the eighteenth century. Sir John Vanbrugh, architect of Blenheim Palace (1705; one of the greatest Baroque structures in England), built a crenellated brick house for himself near Greenwich Park in 1717. Perhaps the most important early work to demonstrate the attractions of the style was Horace Walpole's Strawberry Hill at Richmond upon Thames, on which construction began in 1747.

Early works were hardly notable for their archaeological exactitude. In many, such as John Nash's East Cowes Castle (begun in 1798), Gothic exteriors were merely maskings for Classical interiors. Nor were the massing and disposition of interior space in keeping with the Gothic. It was only in the second half of the nineteenth century that a more precise use evolved.

Pugin's contribution was to make accurate examples of true Gothic architecture available. Published in 1821, *Specimens of Gothic Architecture* (not to be confused with an unsuccessful work of the same title published in 1816) was among the first works to serve as a reliable sourcebook, offering examples that were both well chosen and well rendered. Other titles by Pugin include *Specimens of the Architectural Antiquities of Normandy* (1827), *Examples of Gothic Architecture* (1831) and the present work.

Gothic Ornaments, Selected From Various Buildings in England and France was first published in book form by Preistley & Weale, London, in 1831. The plates, which are individually dated from June 1828 to April 1831, were probably issued separately during that period. The original captions to each plate (omitted here) bore the name of the artist and/or lithographer (when identified), the name of Charles Joseph Hullmandel (printer; 1789–1850), the identification of the subject of the plate (which forms the basis of the present captions) and the identification of Pugin, 105 Great Russell Street, as publisher.

James Duffield Harding (1798–1863; Pugin's fellow member in the Water-Colour Society) is credited as lithographer for plates 1–23, 25, 26, 30, 32 and 38. The artists credited with the original drawings for the plates are Joseph Nash (26–29, 33, 35, 37–39, 41, 44–47, 49–52, 55–58, 60–62, 64–80, 82, 84–89, 91–93, 96–98), Bury (34) and Ferrey (23, 24, 31, 36, 40, 42, 43, 48, 53, 54, 59, 63, 81 [after a drawing by J. Adey Repton], 83, 90, 94, 95, 99, 100). Other plates are not attributed. Plate 82 was reproduced twice: once in black-and-white (reproduced here), once in a hand-colored version (omitted). Some later editions of the book, such as that published by Henry G. Bohn, London, in 1854, featured plates that had been redrawn and lacked the delicacy of touch that makes the originals so attractive.

...

NOTE: In considering scale, readers should bear in mind that the plates of the present edition have been reduced from those of the original by ten percent.

PUGIN'S GOTHIC ORNAMENT

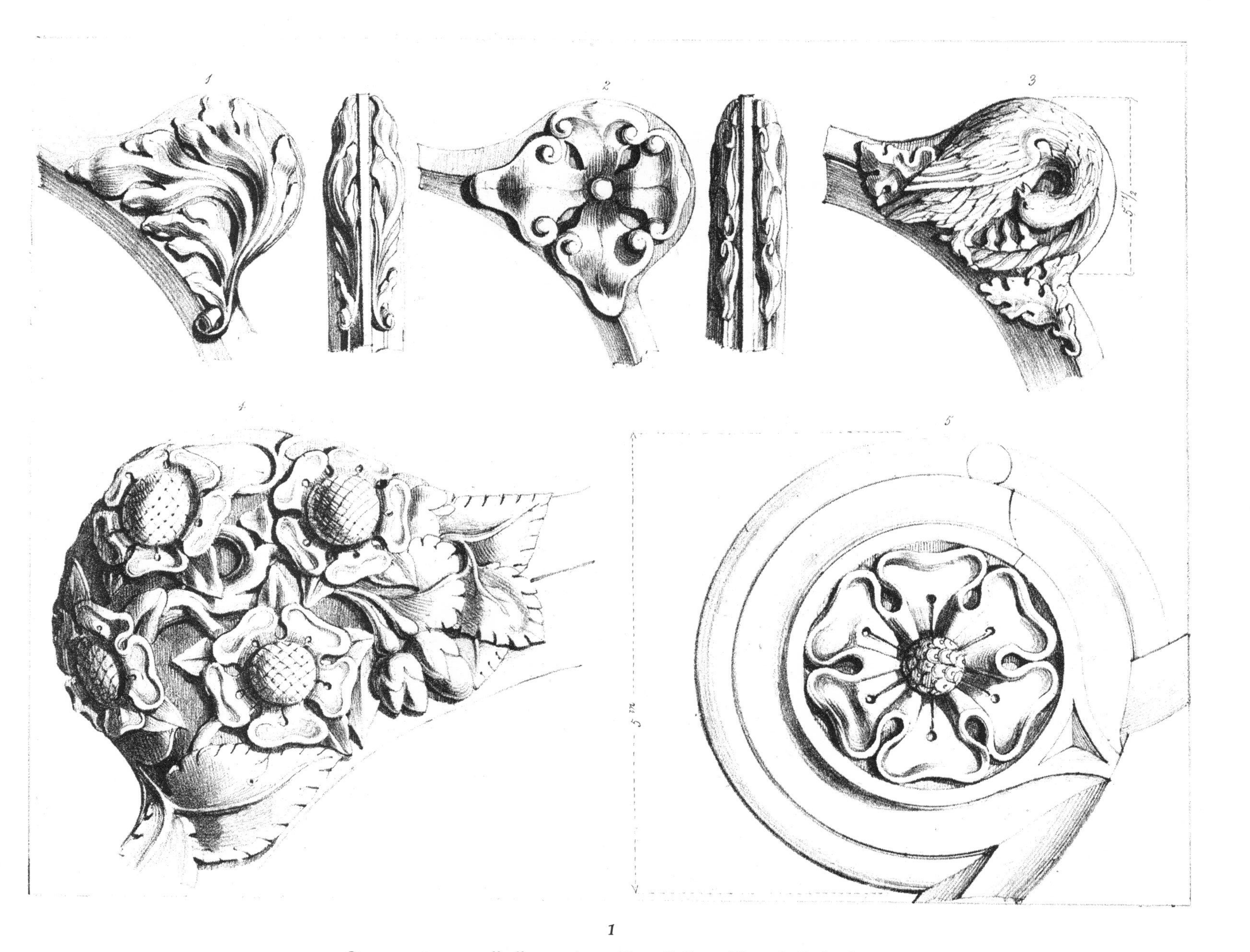

1

Ornaments on stall elbows. (1–4: New College Chapel, Oxford; 5: Beddington Church, Surrey.)

2

Stall finial. (All Souls College Chapel, Oxford.)

3

Ornaments. (The Church of St. Katharine, Tower Hill, London. 1–4: wooden spandrels from stalls; 5: stone ornament from the Duke of Exeter's monument.)

4

Wooden spandrels from stalls. (The Church of St. Katharine, Tower Hill, London.)

5

Stall finial. (All Souls College Chapel, Oxford.)

6

Grotesques from misericords. (New College Chapel, Oxford.)

7

Wooden ornaments from misericords. (All Souls College Chapel, Oxford.)

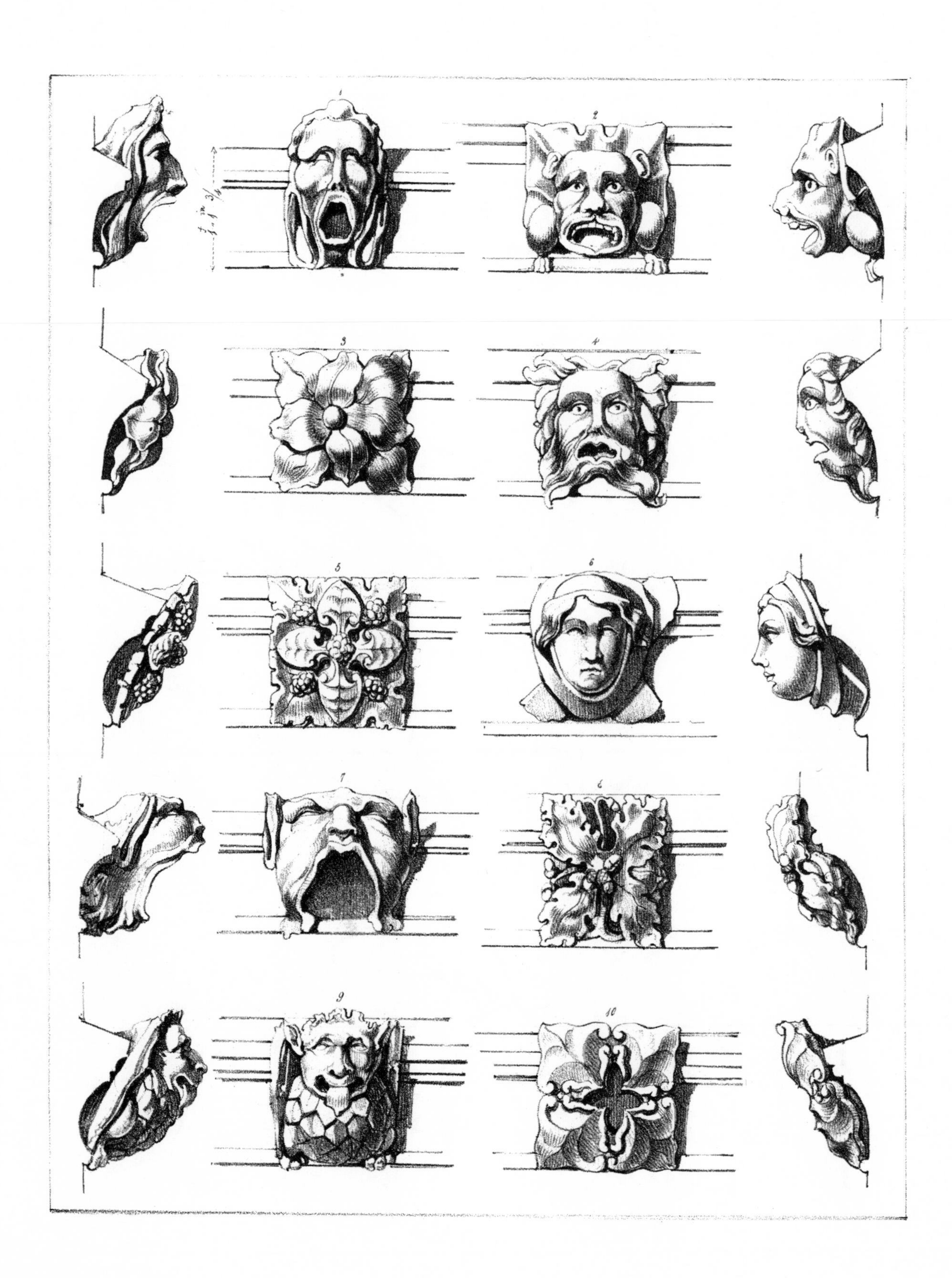

8

Ornaments for stringcourses. (1, 5, 7, 9, 10: Magdalen College, Oxford; 2–4, 6, 8: Merton College Chapel, Oxford.)

9

Ornaments. (Beddington Church, Surrey. 1–4: wooden ornaments from misericords; 5: from the monument of Sir Nicholas Carew.)

10

Stone paterae from basements. (Divinity School, Oxford.)

11

Wooden ornaments from stalls. (New College Chapel, Oxford.)

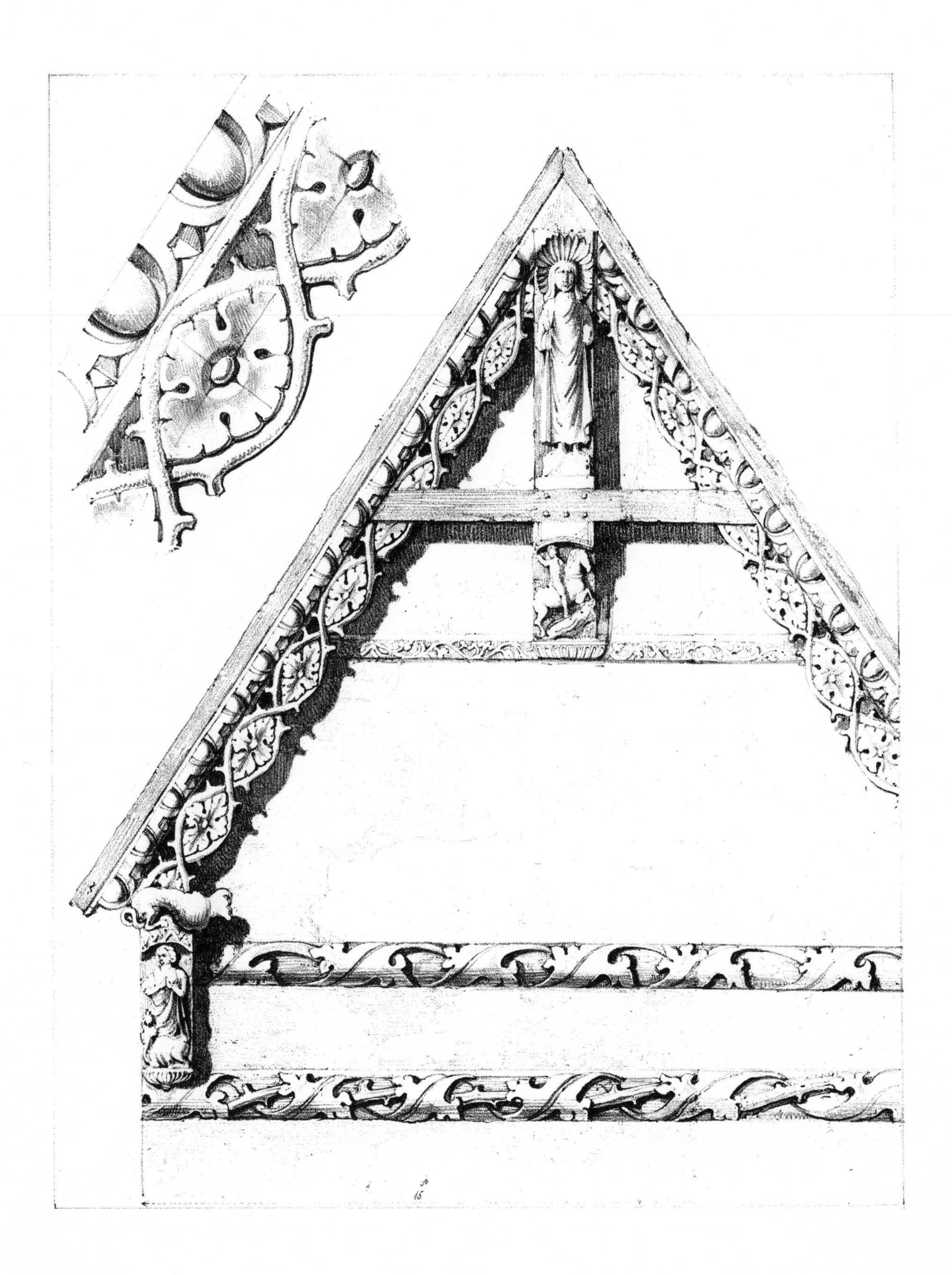

12

Gable. (Rue Tartare, Abbeville.)

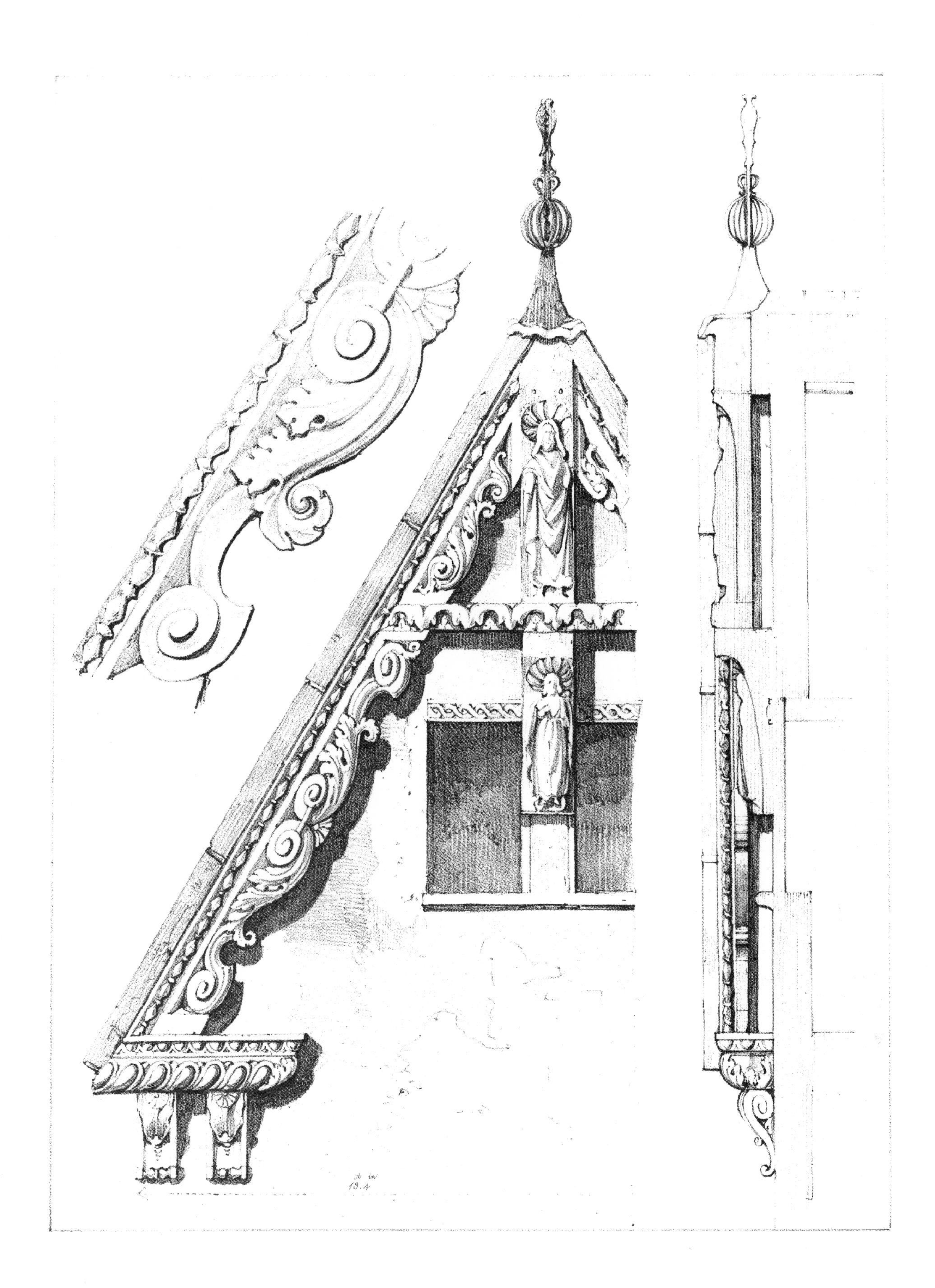

13

Wooden gable. (Marketplace, Abbeville.)

14

Wooden gable. (Rue des Lingères, Abbeville.)

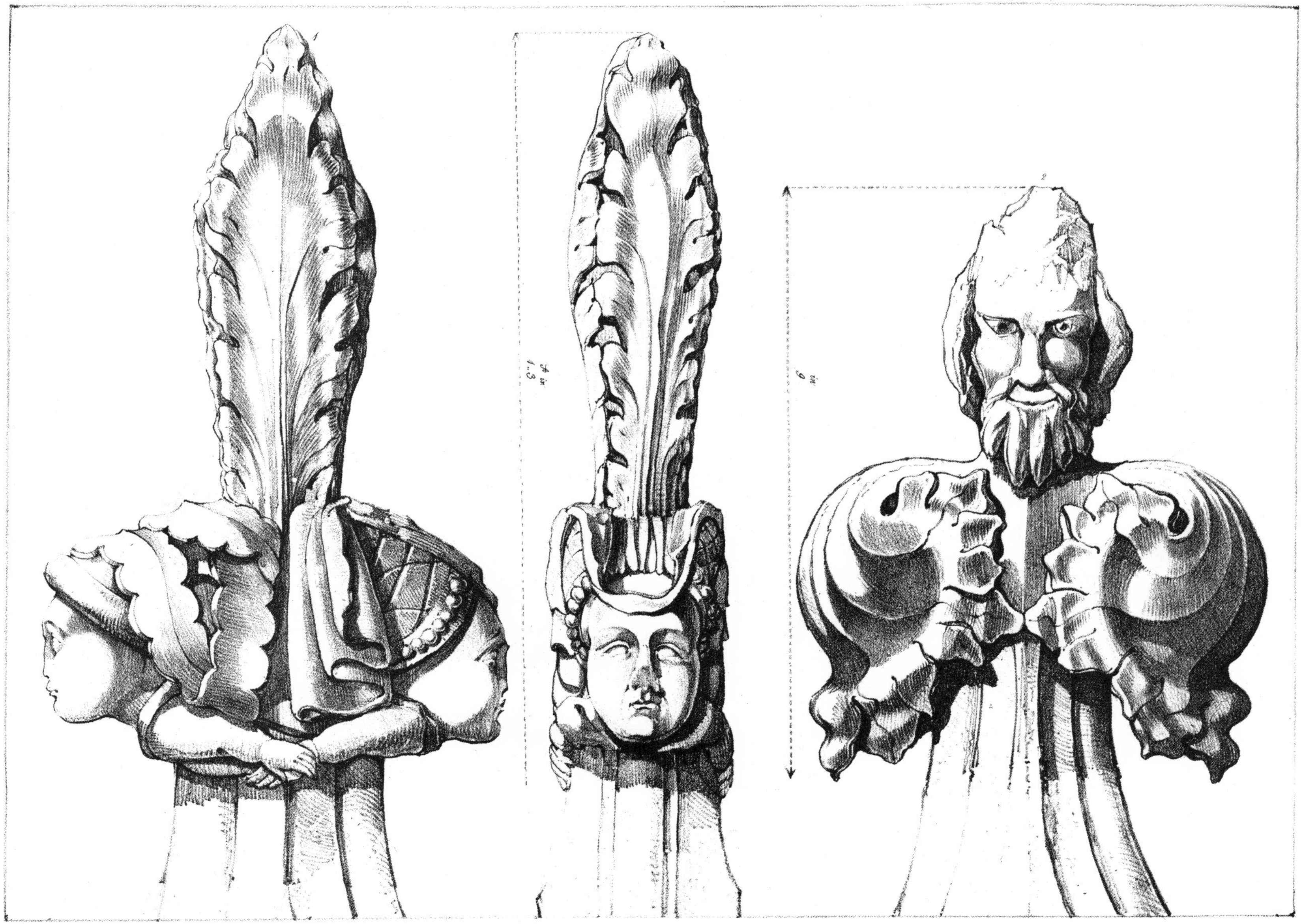

15

Stall finials. (1: St. Mary's Church, Oxford; 2: Wells Church, Norfolk.)

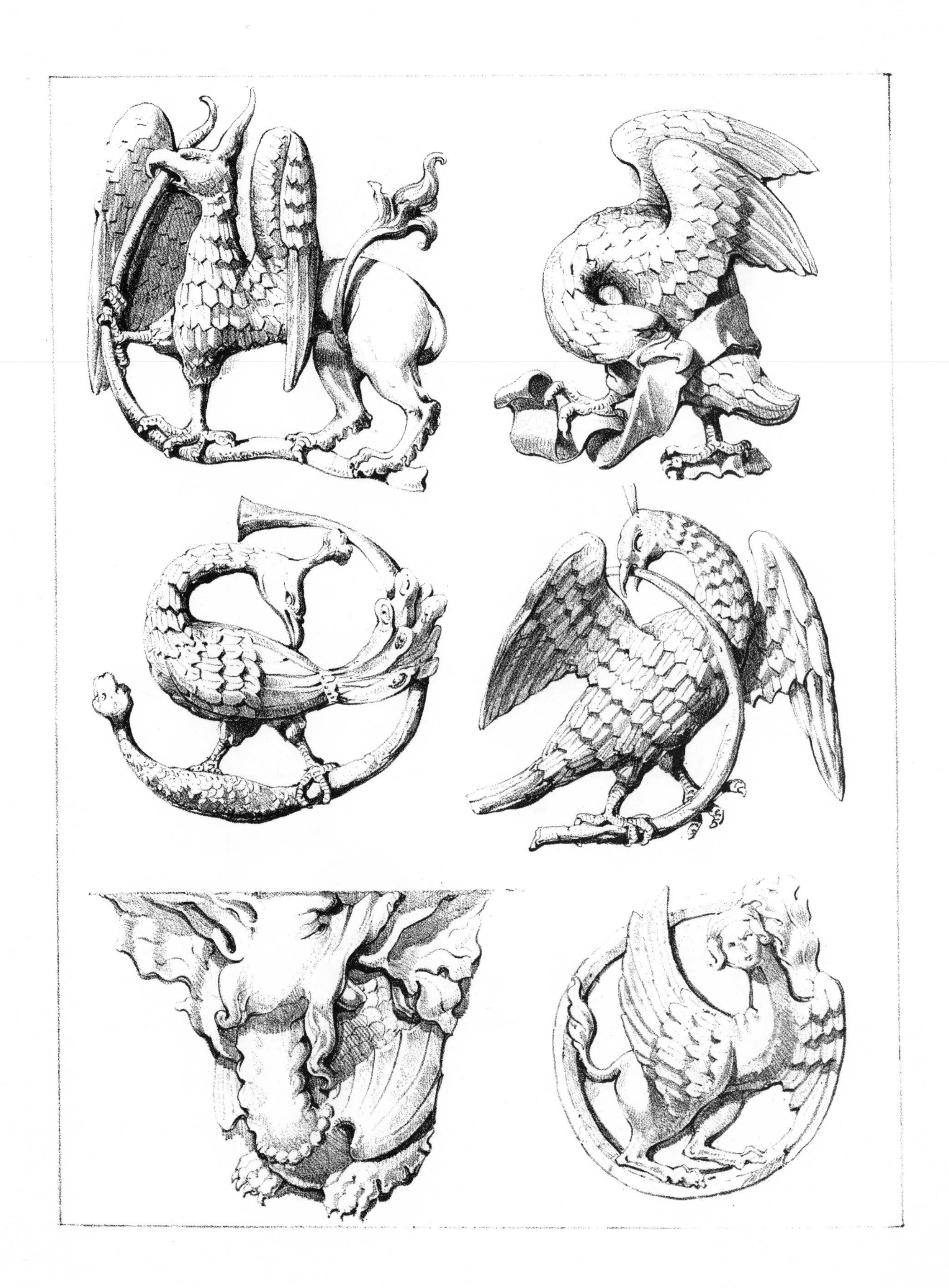

16

Wooden ornaments. (New College Chapel, Oxford.)

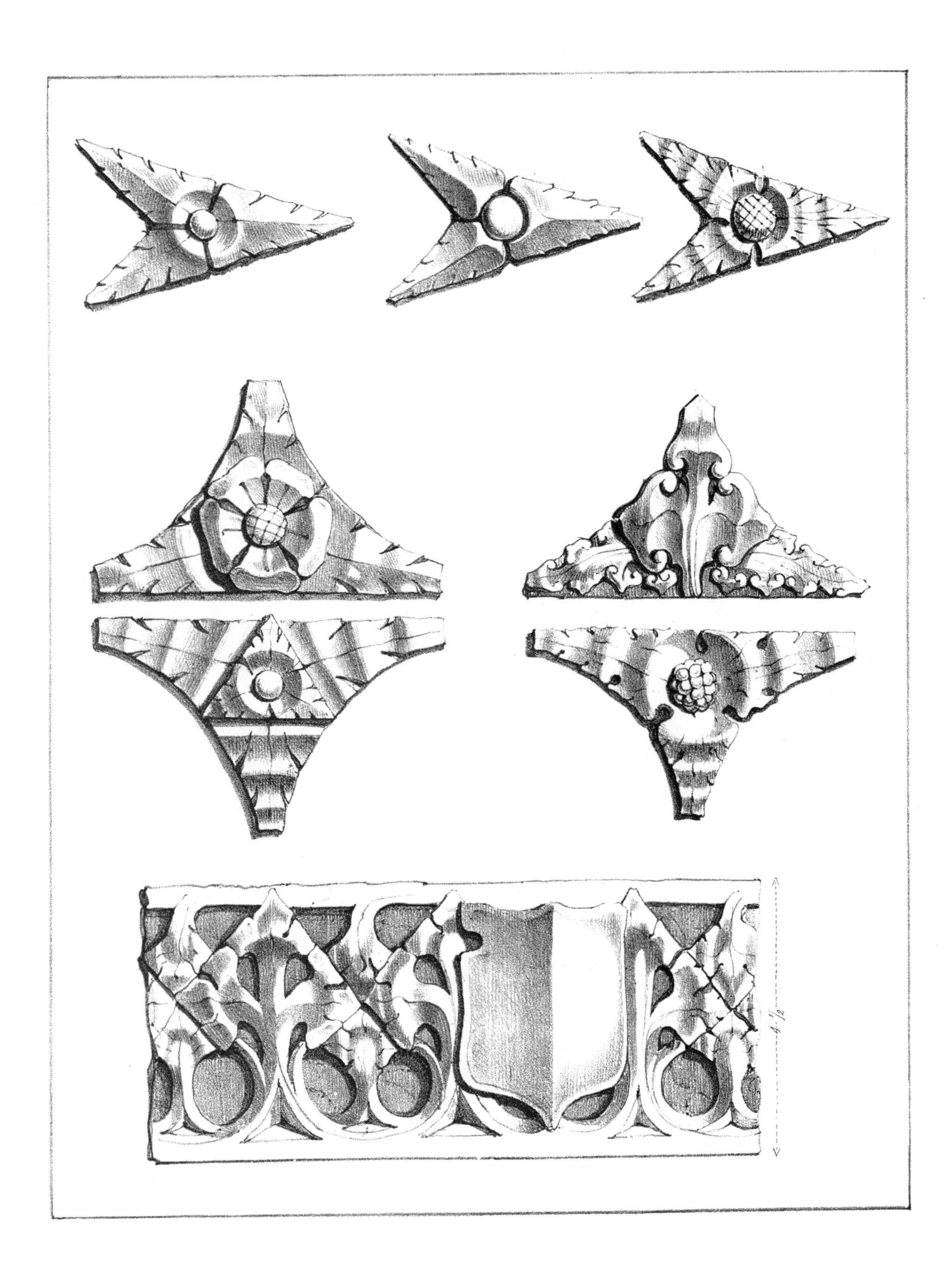

17

Wooden ornaments. (New Walsingham Church, Norfolk.)

18

Stone ornaments. (1, 2: Rouen Cathedral; 3: Beddington Church, Surrey.)

Wooden ornaments. (New Walsingham Church, Norfolk.)

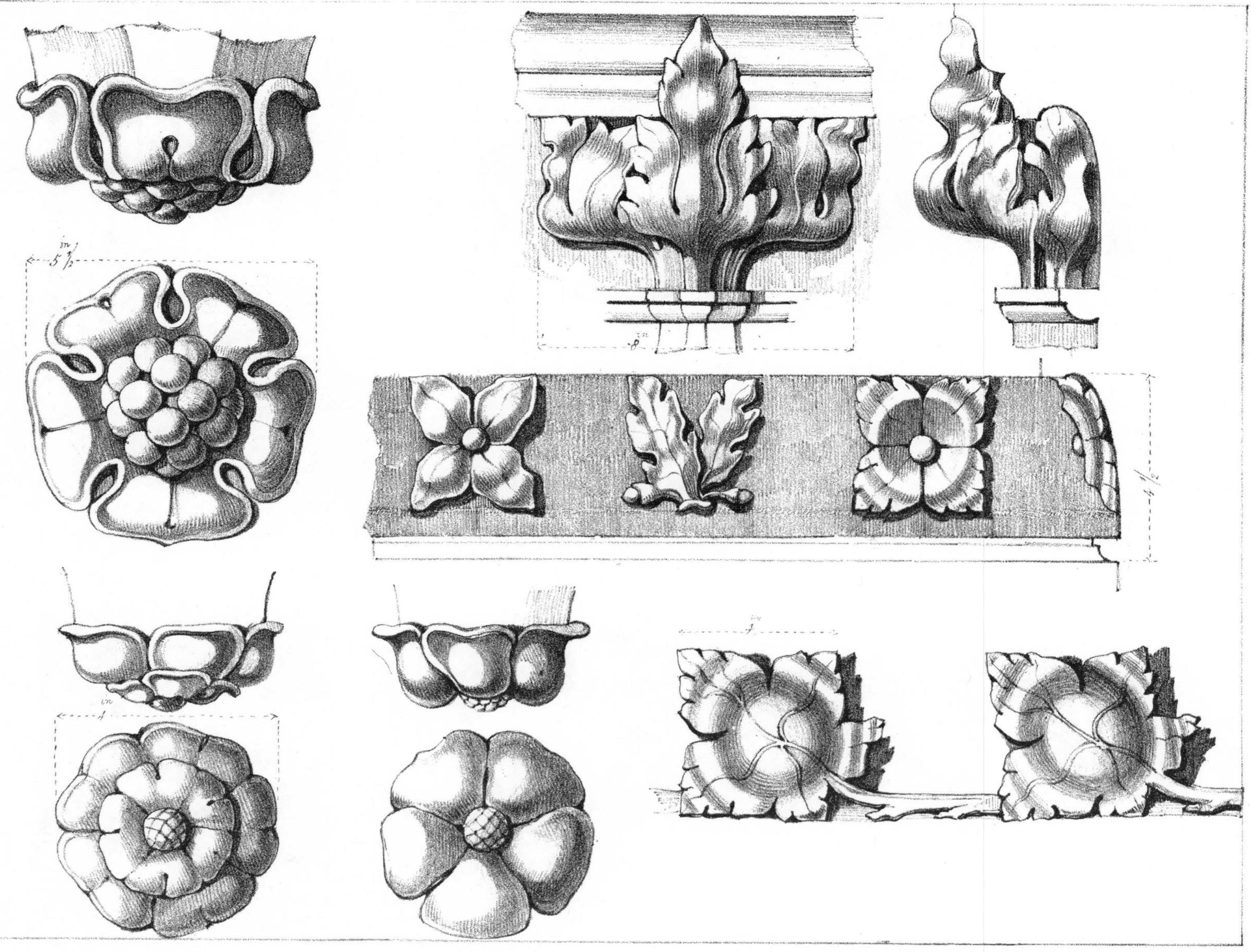

20

Stone ornaments. (Fakenham Church, Norfolk.)

21

Wooden gable. (Eltham Palace, Kent.)

22

Wooden gable. (Rue de la Hucherie, Abbeville.)

23

Wooden ornaments. (Wells Church, Norfolk.)

24

Wooden tracery. (From the author's collection.)

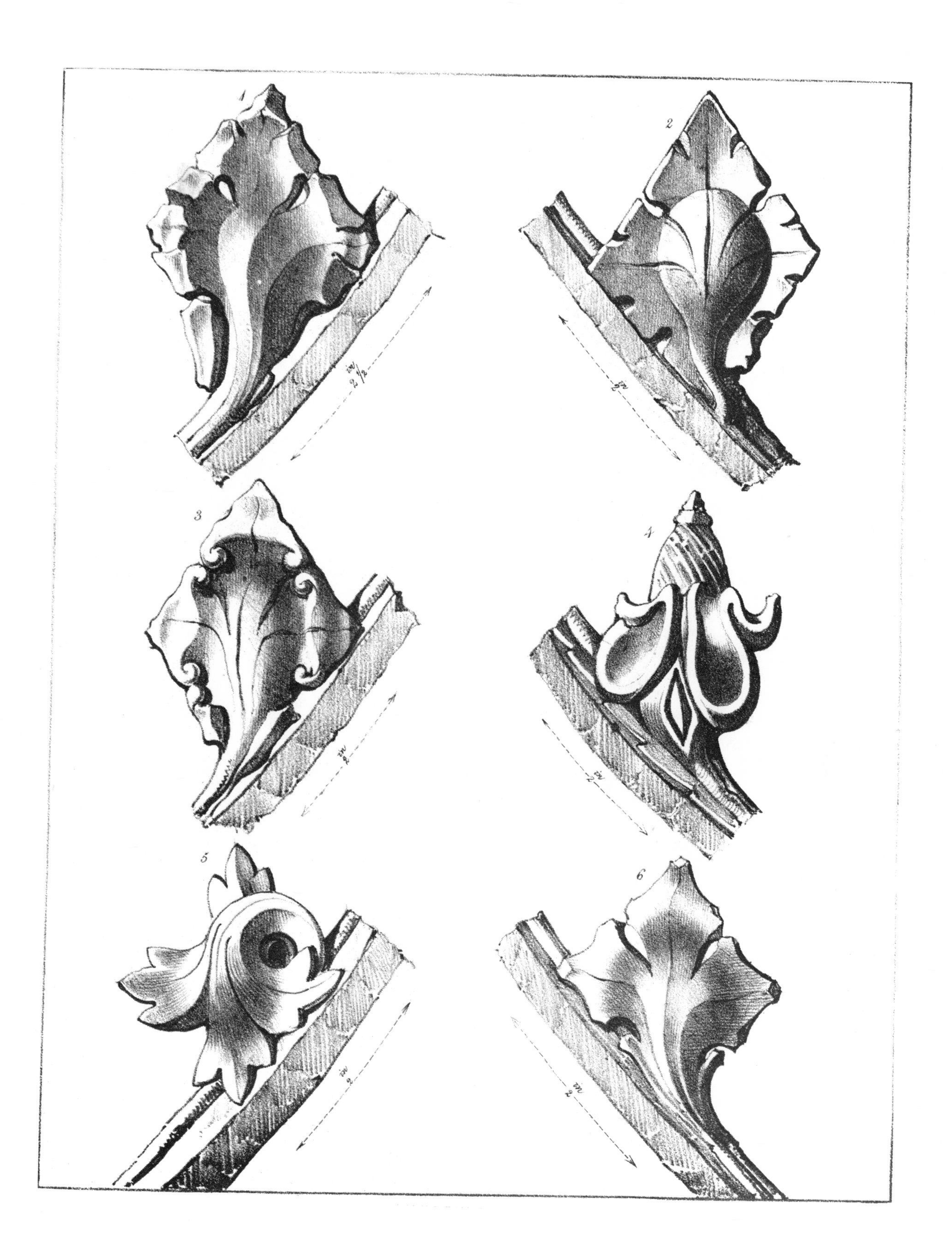

25

Wooden crockets. (1–4: Merton College, Oxford; 5: the Abbey of St. Amand, Rouen.)

26

Stone stringcourses. (Winchester Cathedral.)

27

Wooden ornaments. (1: north door, Rouen Cathedral; 2: stringcourse, chapel, Archbishop's Palace, Croydon.)

28

Stone stringcourses. (1: *Winchester Cathedral*; 2, 3: All Souls College, Oxford.)

29

Stone paterae. (1, 2: Winchester Cathedral; 3, 4: Duke of Exeter's monument, St. Katharine's Church, Tower Hill, London.)

30

Gable. (Eltham Palace, Kent.)

31

Stone finials. (Winchester Cathedral.)

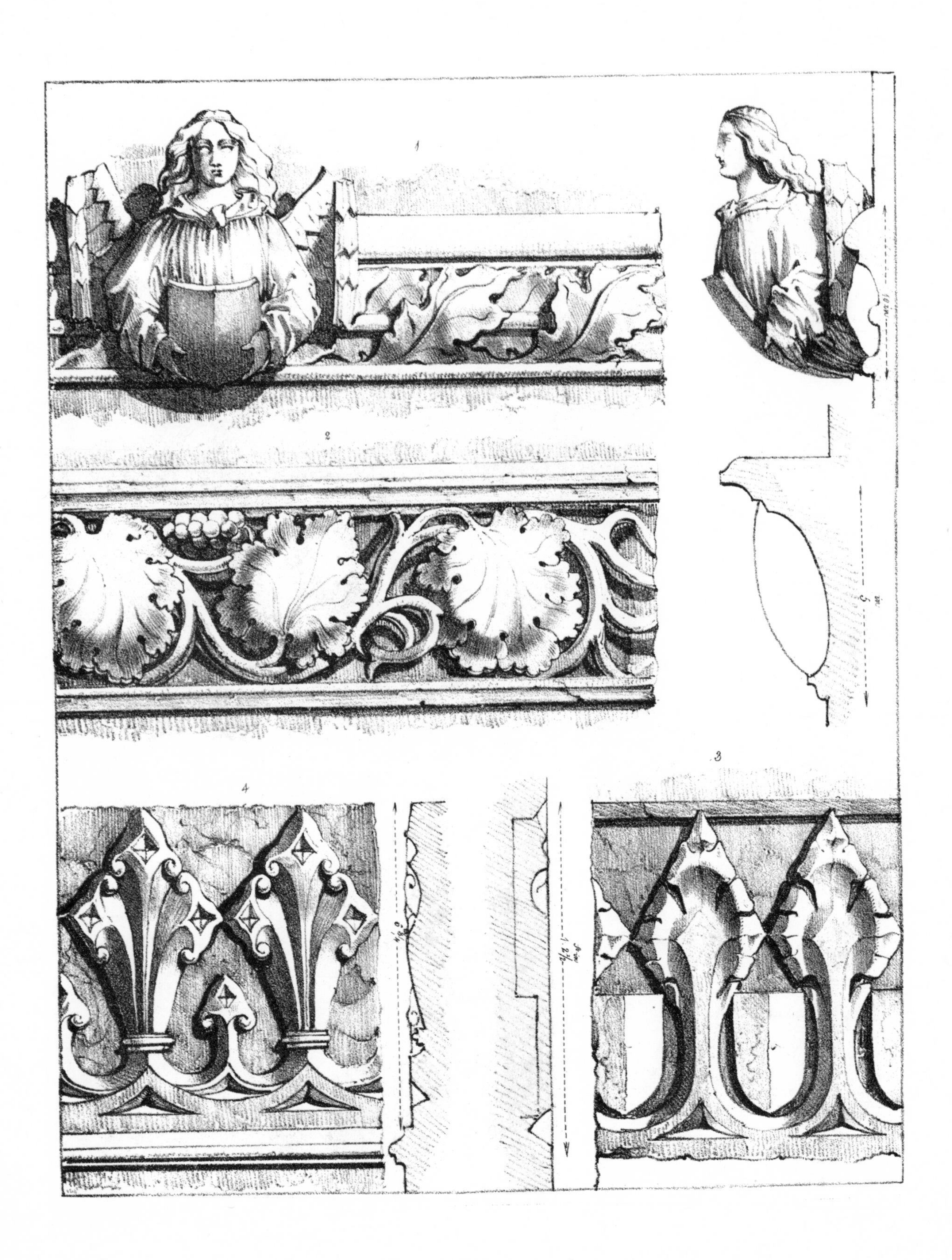

32

Stone stringcourses. (1: St. Mary's Church, Oxford; 2: the Church of Arques, Normandy; 3: East Barsham, Norfolk; 4: Beddington Church, Surrey.)

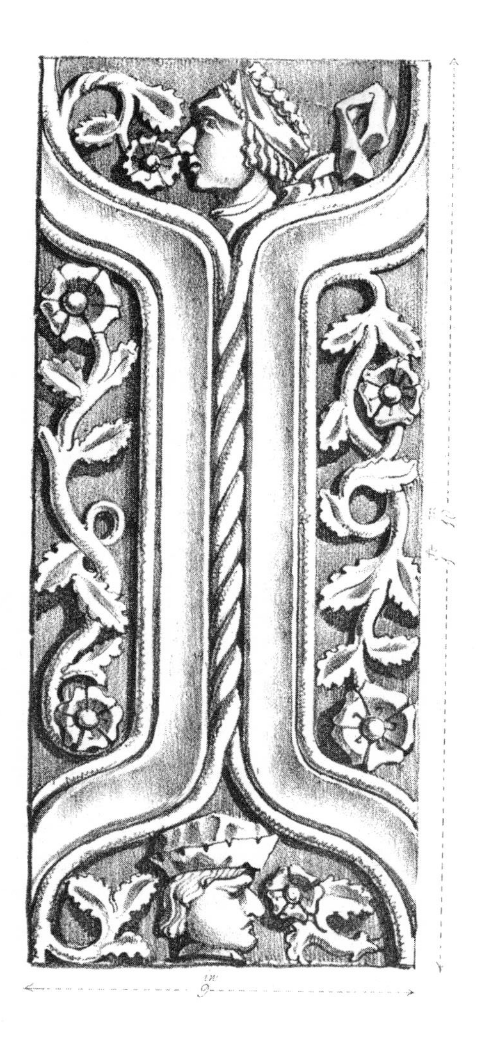

33

Oak panels. (Manor House, Beddington, Surrey.)

34

Stone paterae. (1: Waynflete's monument, Winchester Cathedral; 2, 3: Duke of Exeter's monument, St. Katharine's Church, Tower Hill, London.)

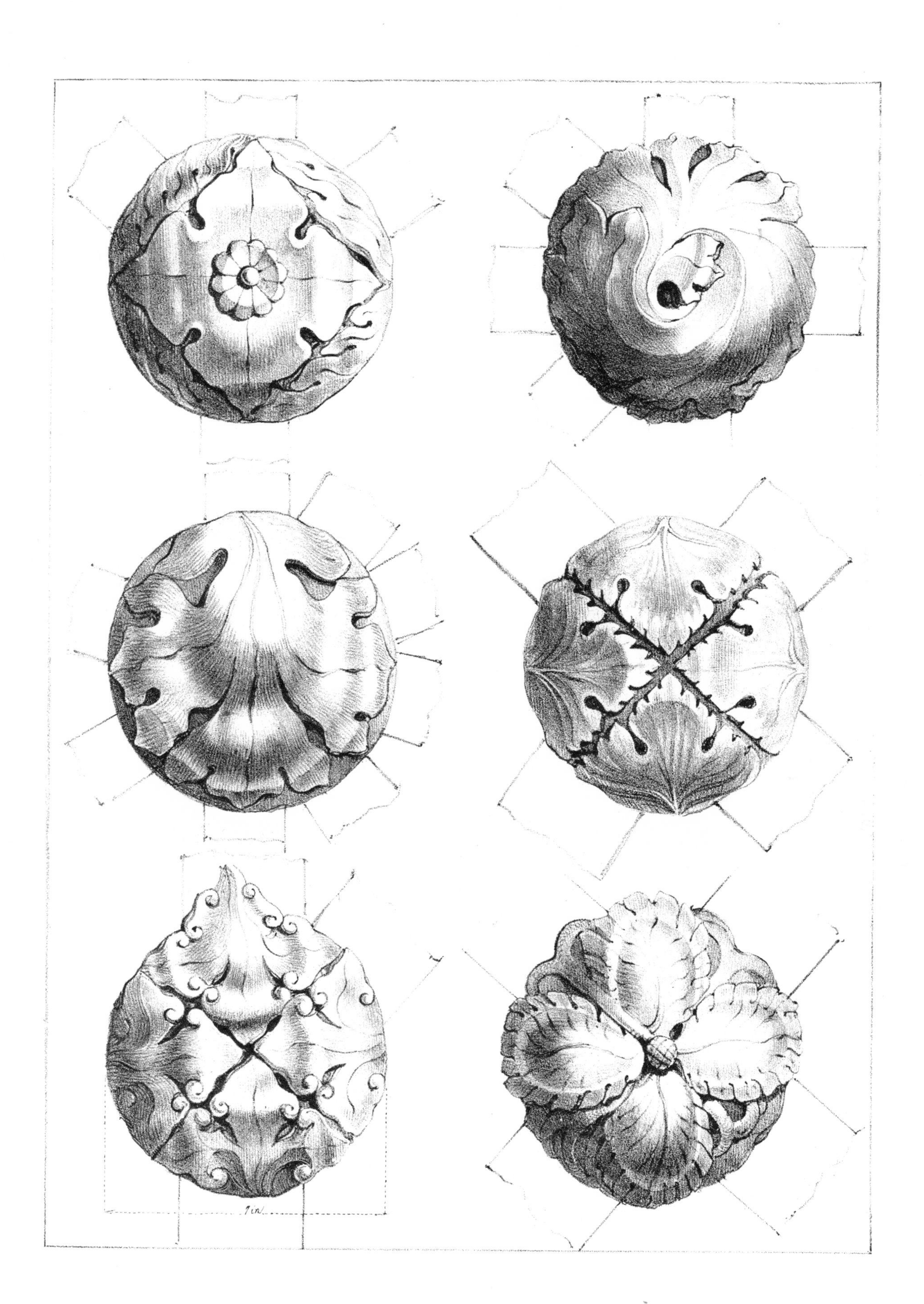

35

Stone bosses. (Eltham Palace, Kent.)

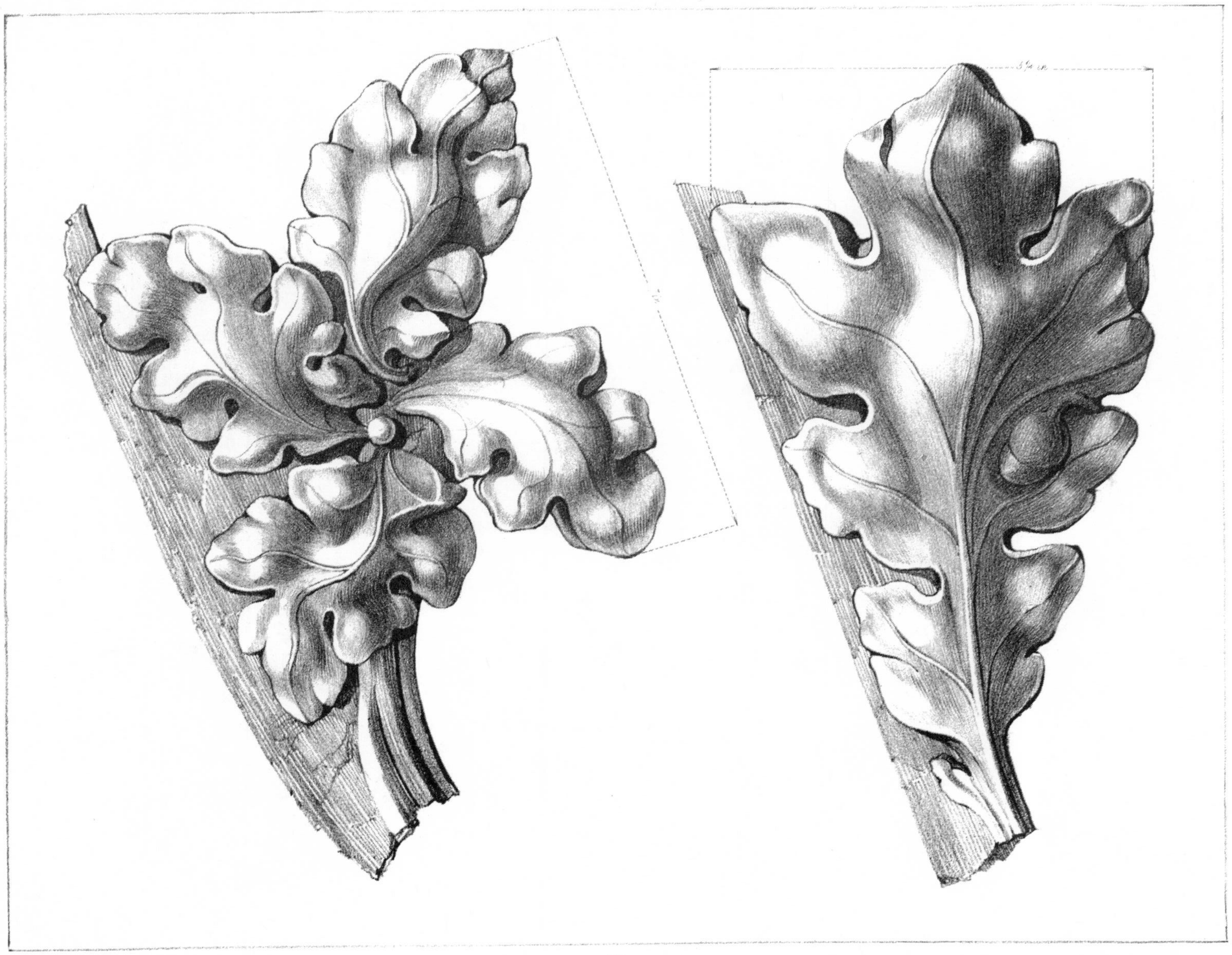

36

Crockets. (Waynflete's monument, Winchester Cathedral.)

37

Ornaments. (1, 3: stone spandrels, Winchester Cathedral; 2, 4: wooden ornaments, Henry VII Chapel, Westminster Abbey.)

38

Wooden gable. (Rue de la Hucherie, Abbeville.)

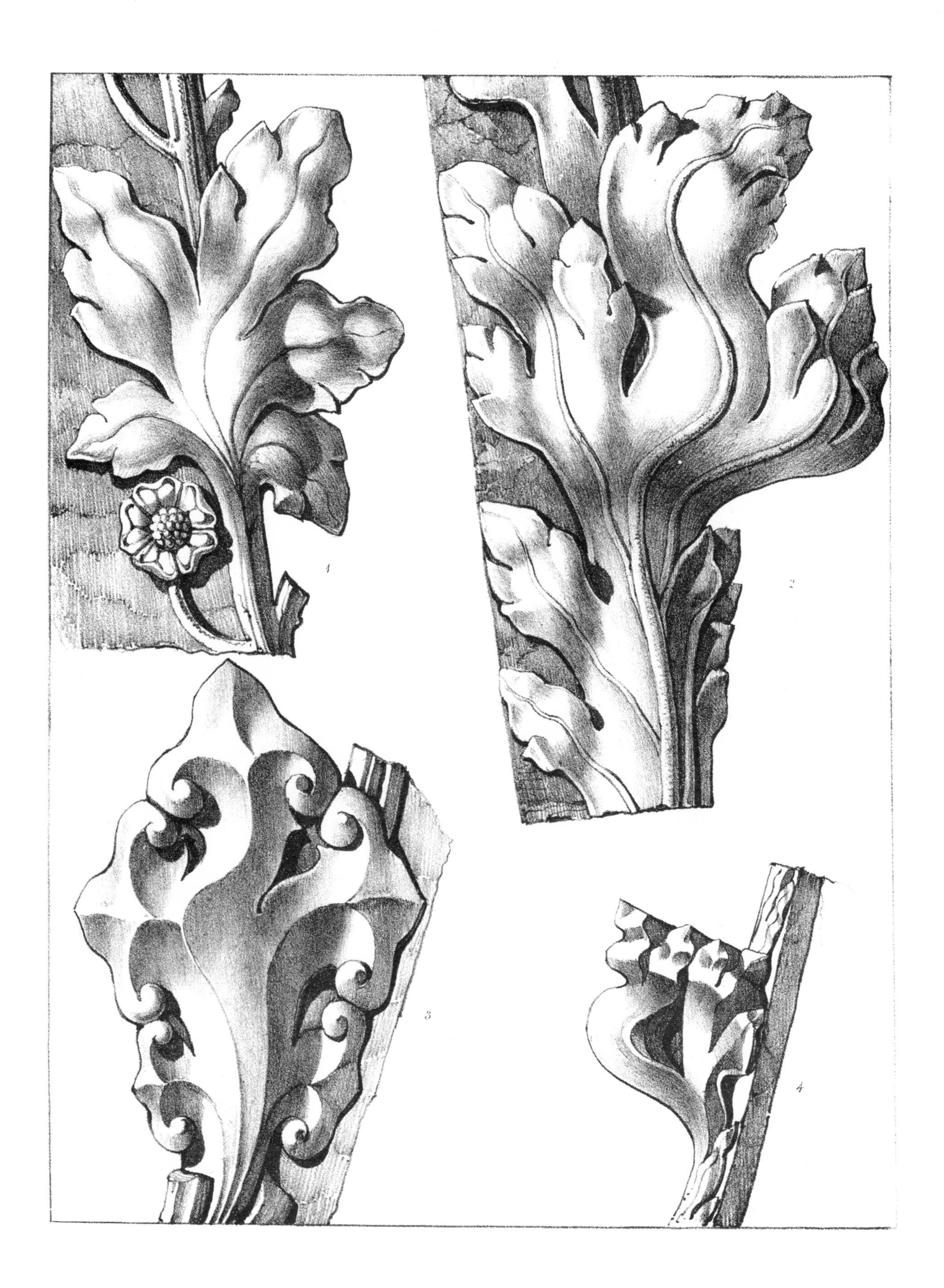

39

Crockets. (1, 2: Winchester Cathedral; 3, 4: Duke of Exeter's monument, St. Katharine's Church, Tower Hill, London.)

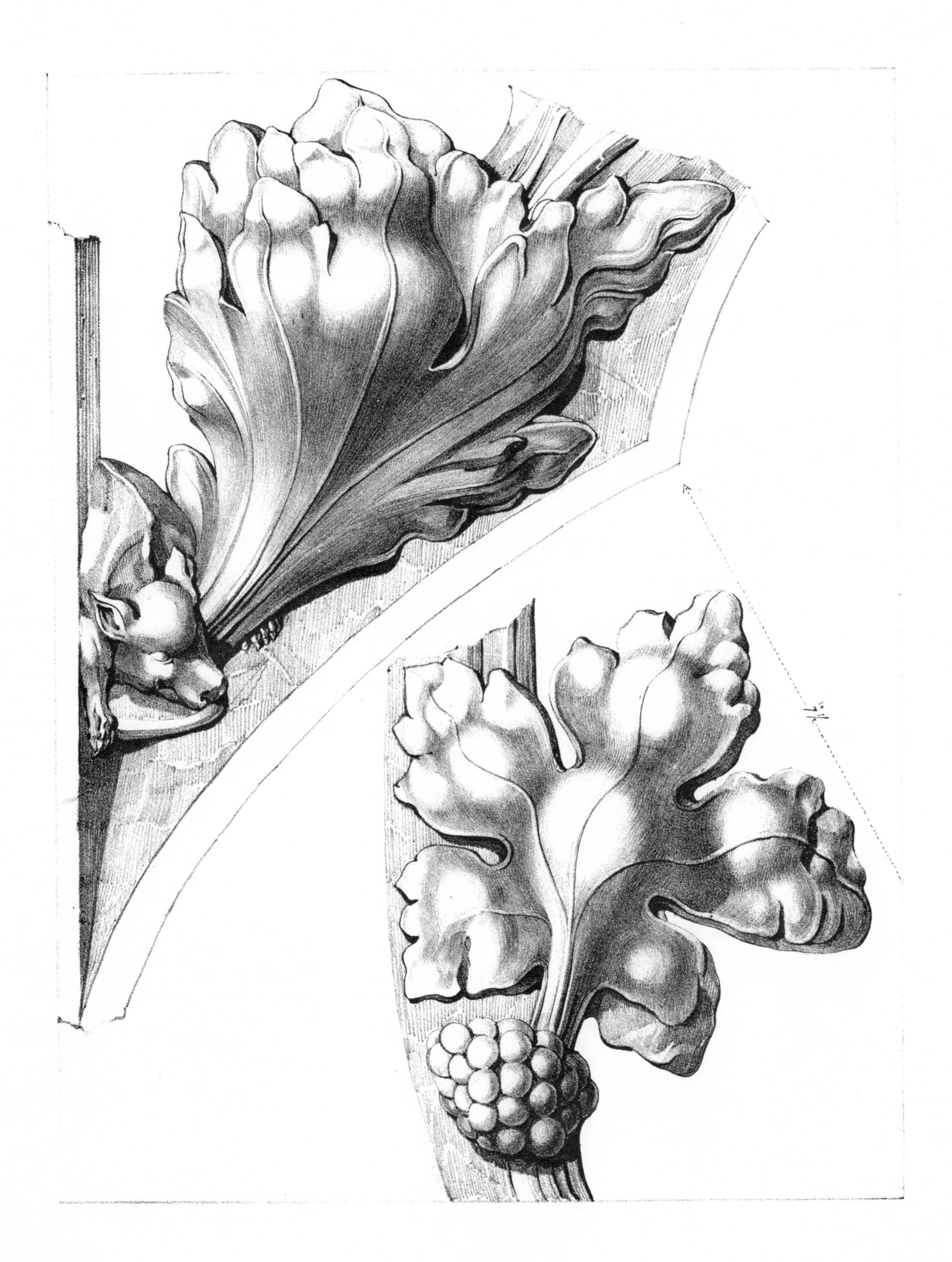

40

Crockets. (Waynflete's monument, Winchester Cathedral.)

41

Stone ornaments. (1: stringcourse, Croydon Church, Surrey; 2: paterae, Salisbury Cathedral.)

42

Ornaments. (1: stone patera, Westminster Abbey; 2, 3: stone patera and stringcourse, Winchester Cathedral.)

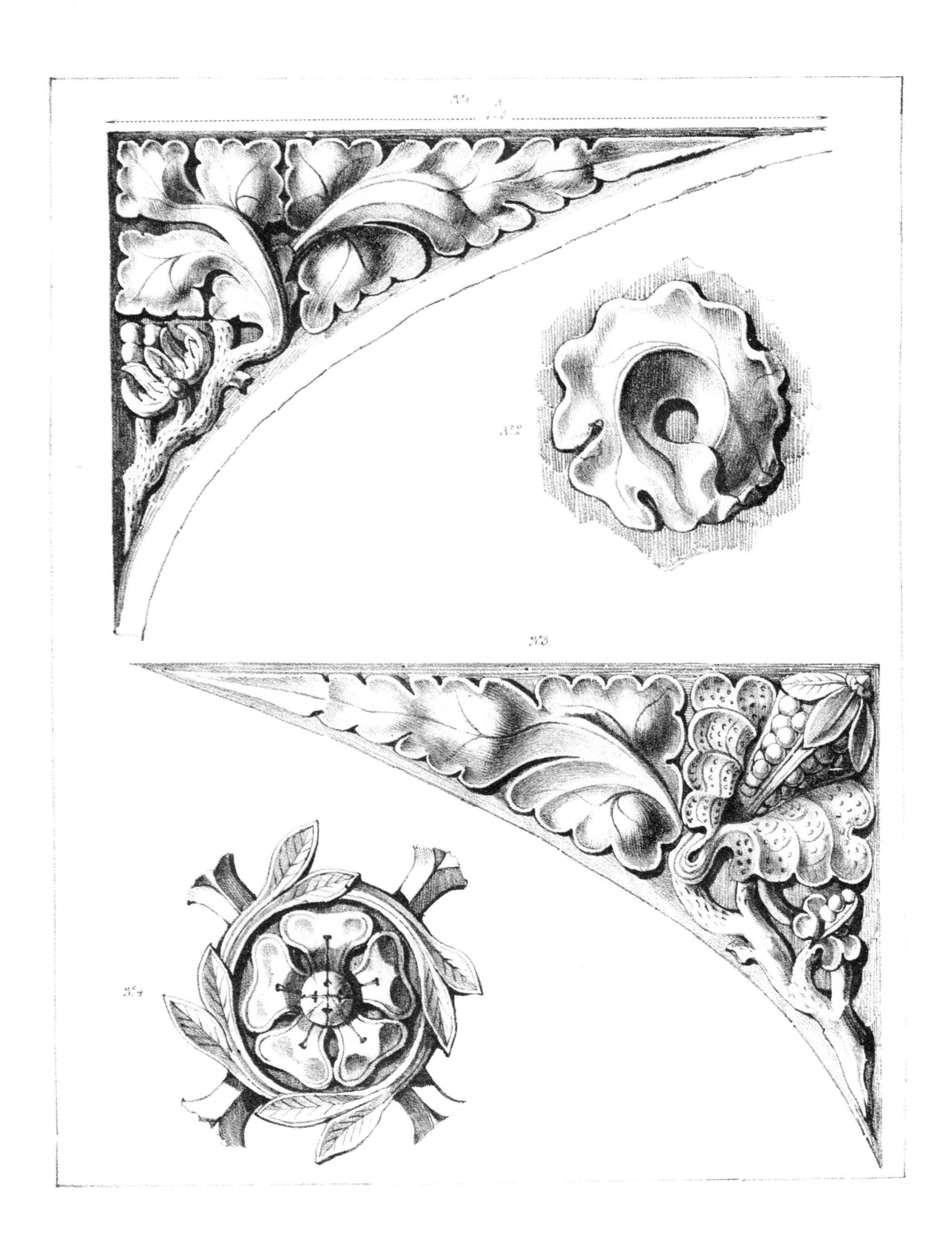

43

Ornaments. (1, 3: spandrels, St. Albans Church, Hertfordshire; 2, 4: wooden paterae, Wells Church, Norfolk.)

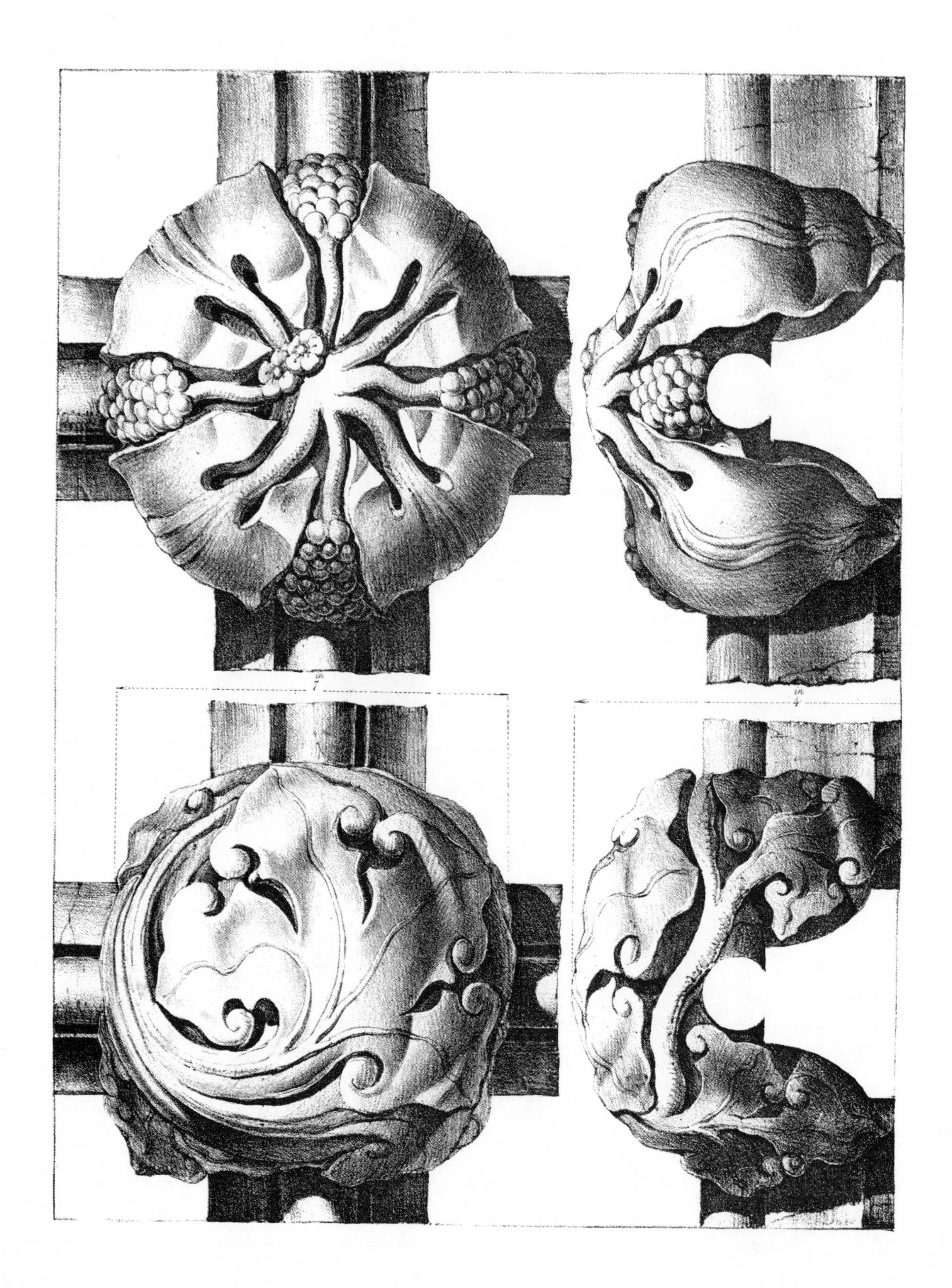

44

Stone bosses. (York Minster.)

45

Stone capitals. (York Minster.)

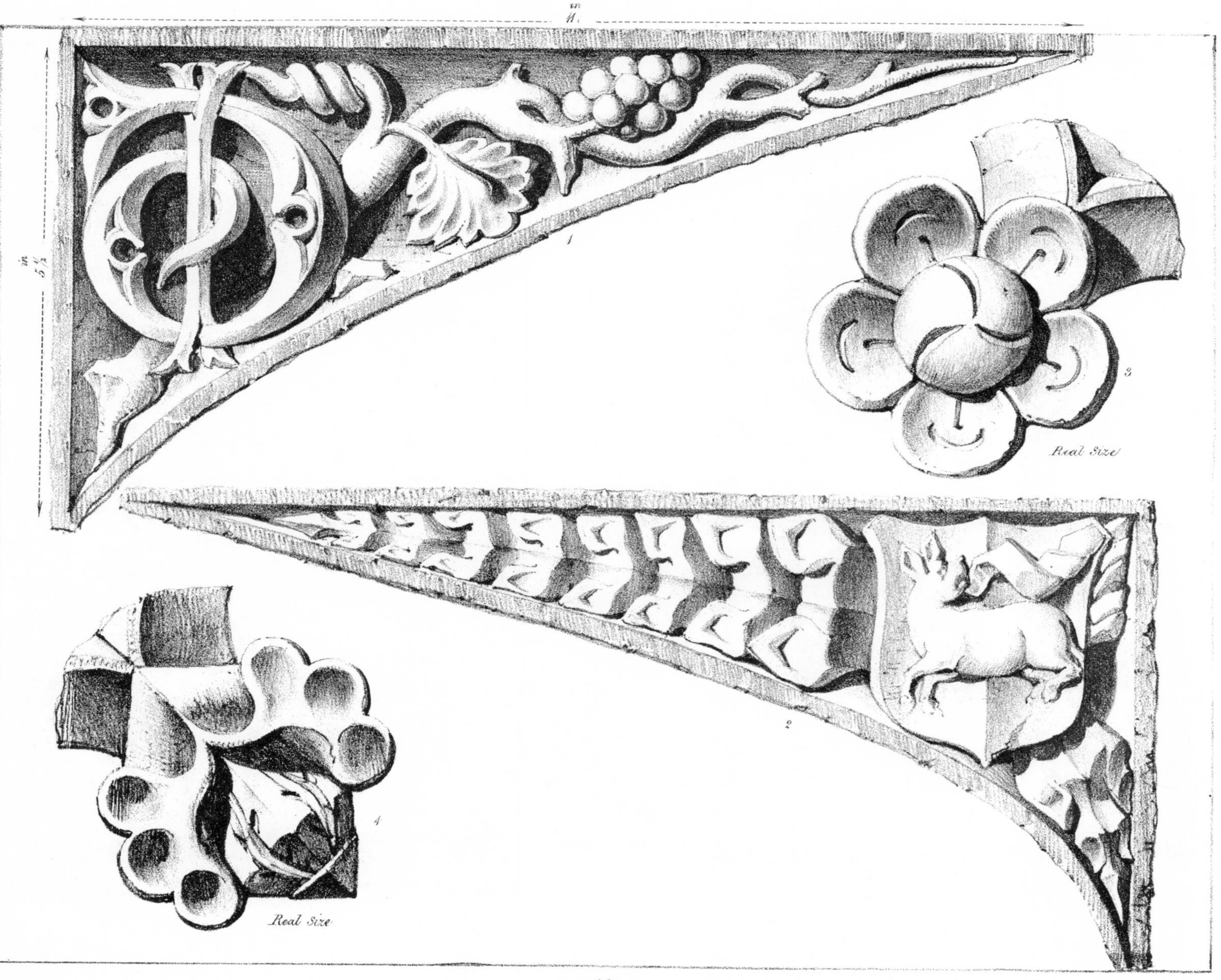

46

Ornaments. (Drapers Chapel, Christchurch, Hampshire. 1, 2: stone spandrels; 3, 4: wooden ornaments from choir stalls.)

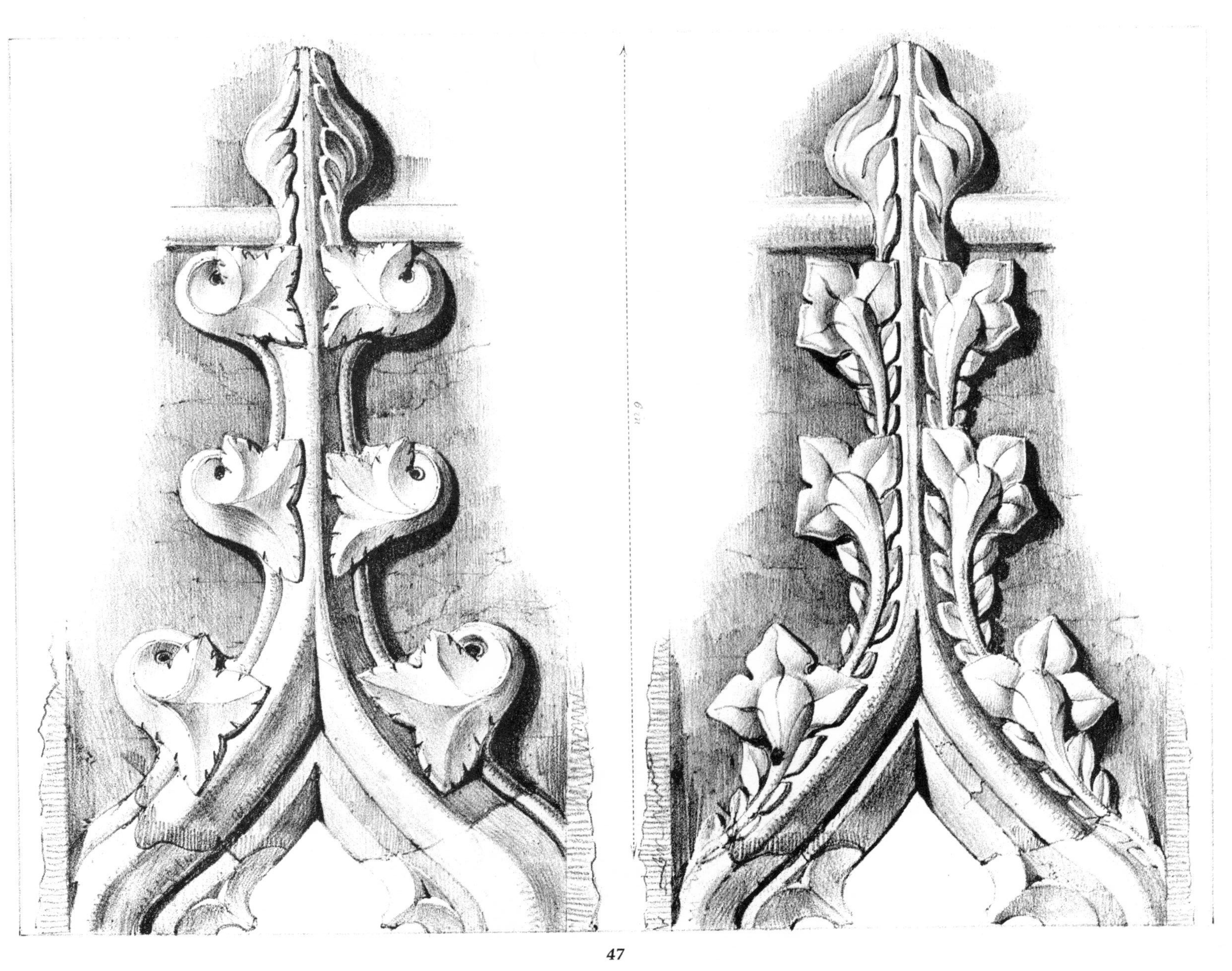

47

Stone crockets. (Countess of Salisbury's Chantry, Christchurch, Hampshire.)

48

Wooden gable. (New Brentford, Middlesex.)

49

Wooden stringcourses. (1: Aldenham Abbey; 2, 3: Ely Cathedral; 4: Westminster Abbey.)

50

Wooden ornaments. (Door, north transept, Rouen Cathedral.)

51

Buttresses. (Corner of a monument, Spilsby Church, Lincolnshire.)

52

Oak panels. (Beddington Manor House, Surrey.)

53

Oak panel. (From the author's collection.)

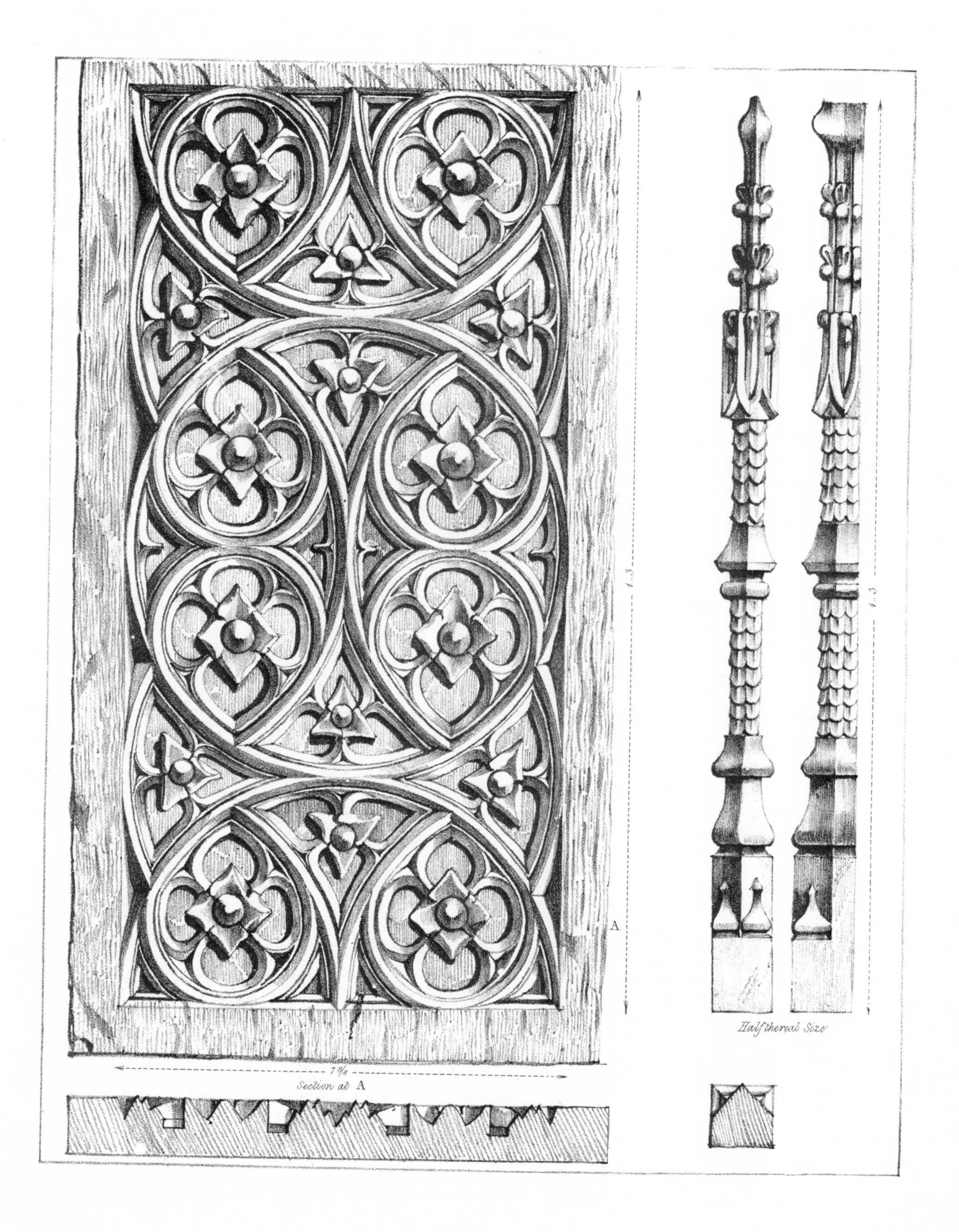

54

Wooden ornaments. (Oak panel, Abbey of St. Amand, Rouen; pinnacle from screen, Church of Arques.)

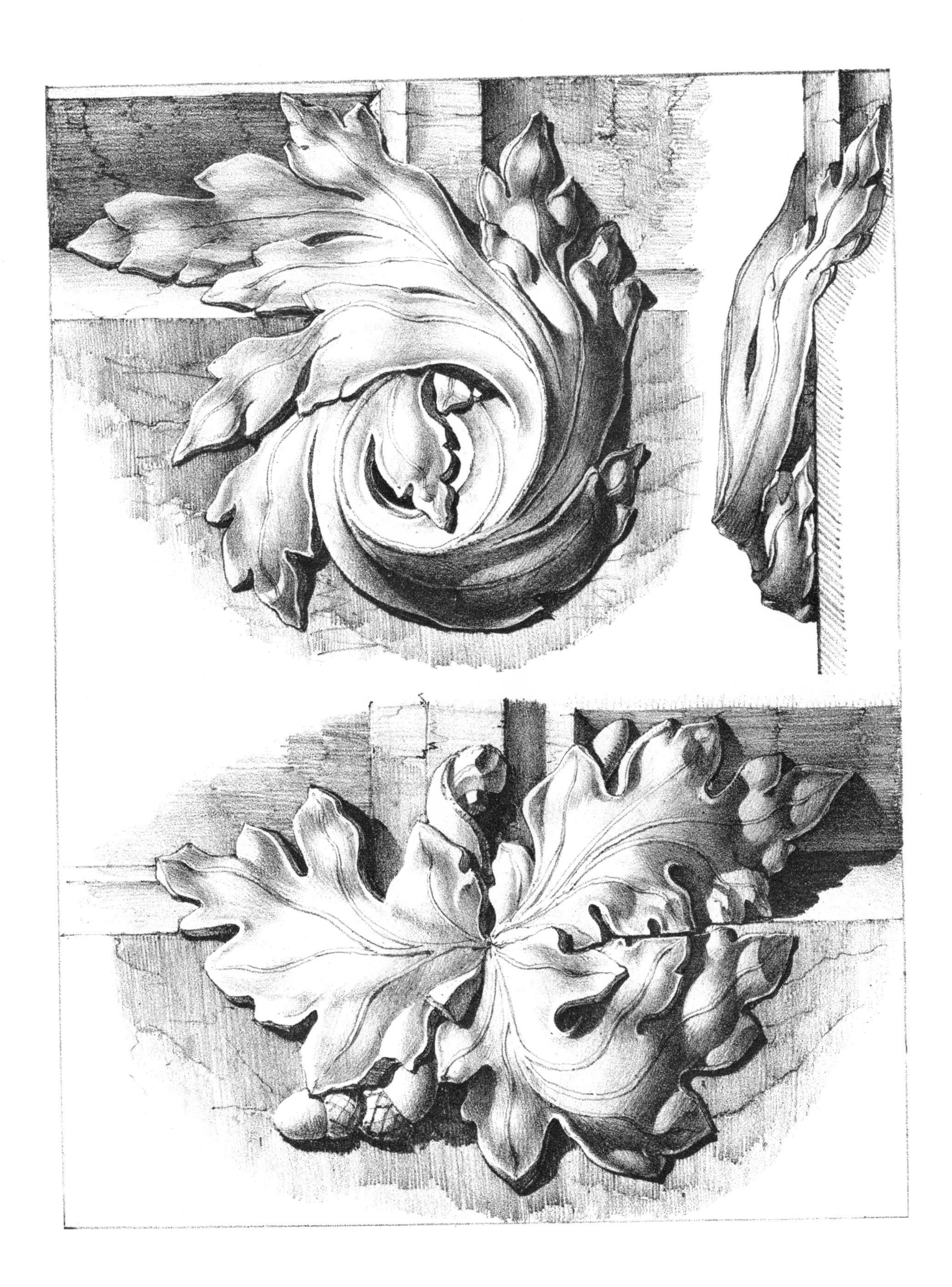

55

Stone ornaments. (Fox's monument, Winchester Cathedral.)

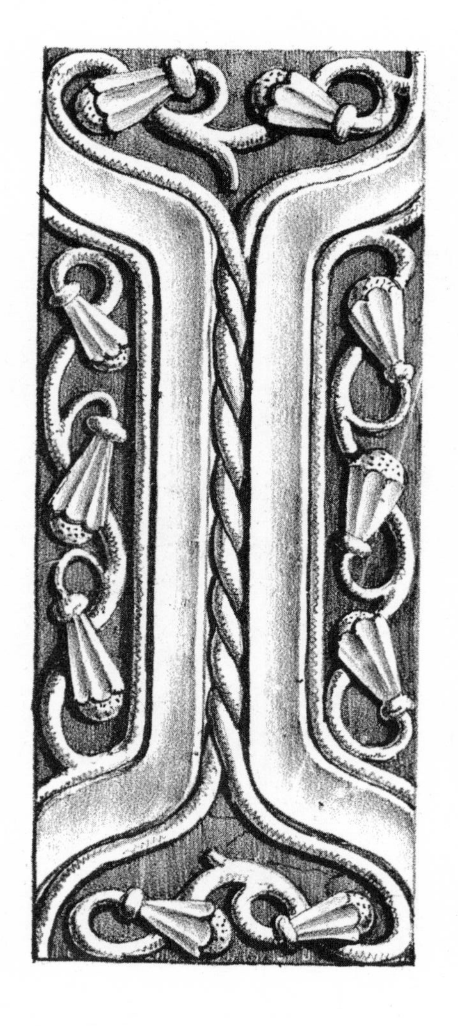

56

Oak panels. (Beddington Manor House, Surrey.)

57

Stone stringcourses. (1: York Minster; 2: Westminster Abbey.)

6 in

6 in

Plans

58

Stone brackets. (York Minster.)

59

Gable. (High Street, Rochester.)

Parts of stone canopies. (1: Speaker's Apartment, Westminster; 2: York Minster.)

61

Stone crowns. (1: Duke Humphrey's monument, Abbot Ramrydge's Chantry, St. Albans Abbey.)

62

Stone stringcourses. (Abbot Ramrydge's Chantry, St. Albans Abbey.)

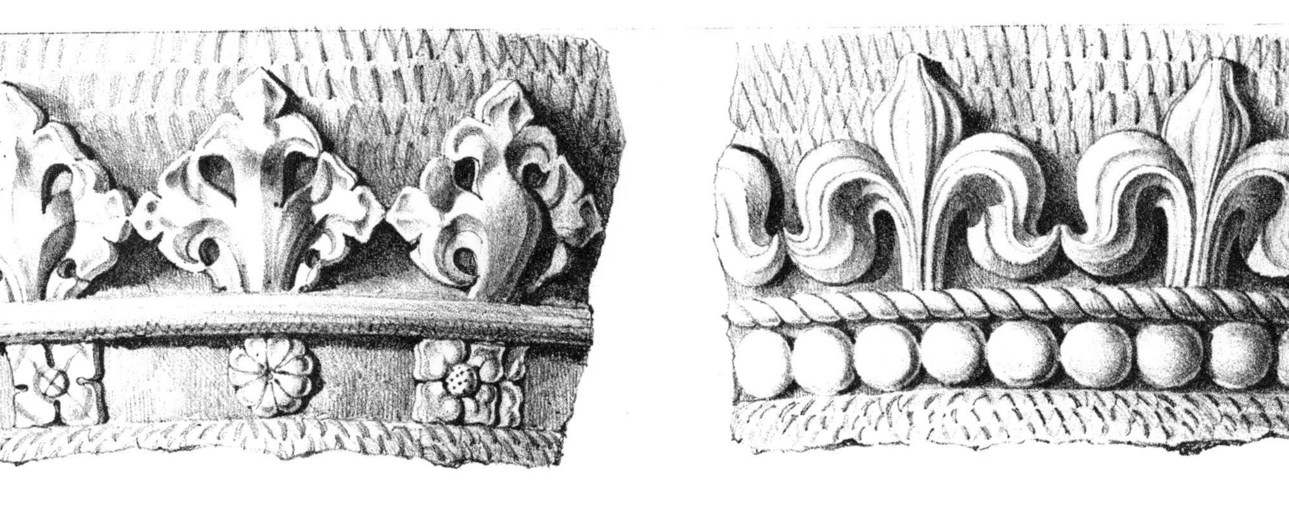

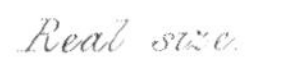

63

Stone crowns. (Abbot Ramrydge's Chantry, St. Albans Abbey.)

64

Stone paterae. (Abbot Ramrydge's Chantry, St. Albans Abbey.)

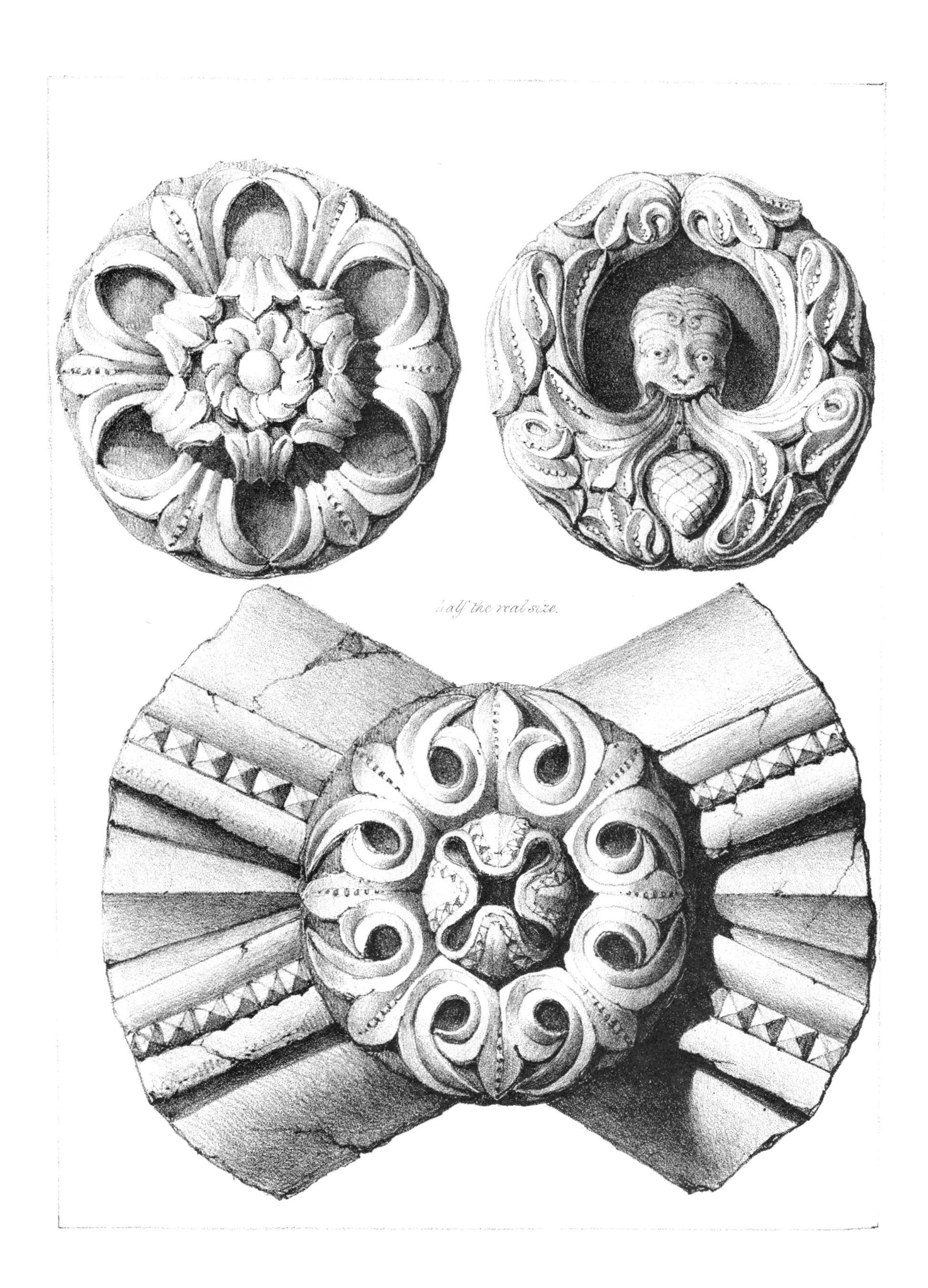

65

Stone bosses. (Soffit of the three entrance arches, Chapter House, St. George de Boucherville, near Rouen.)

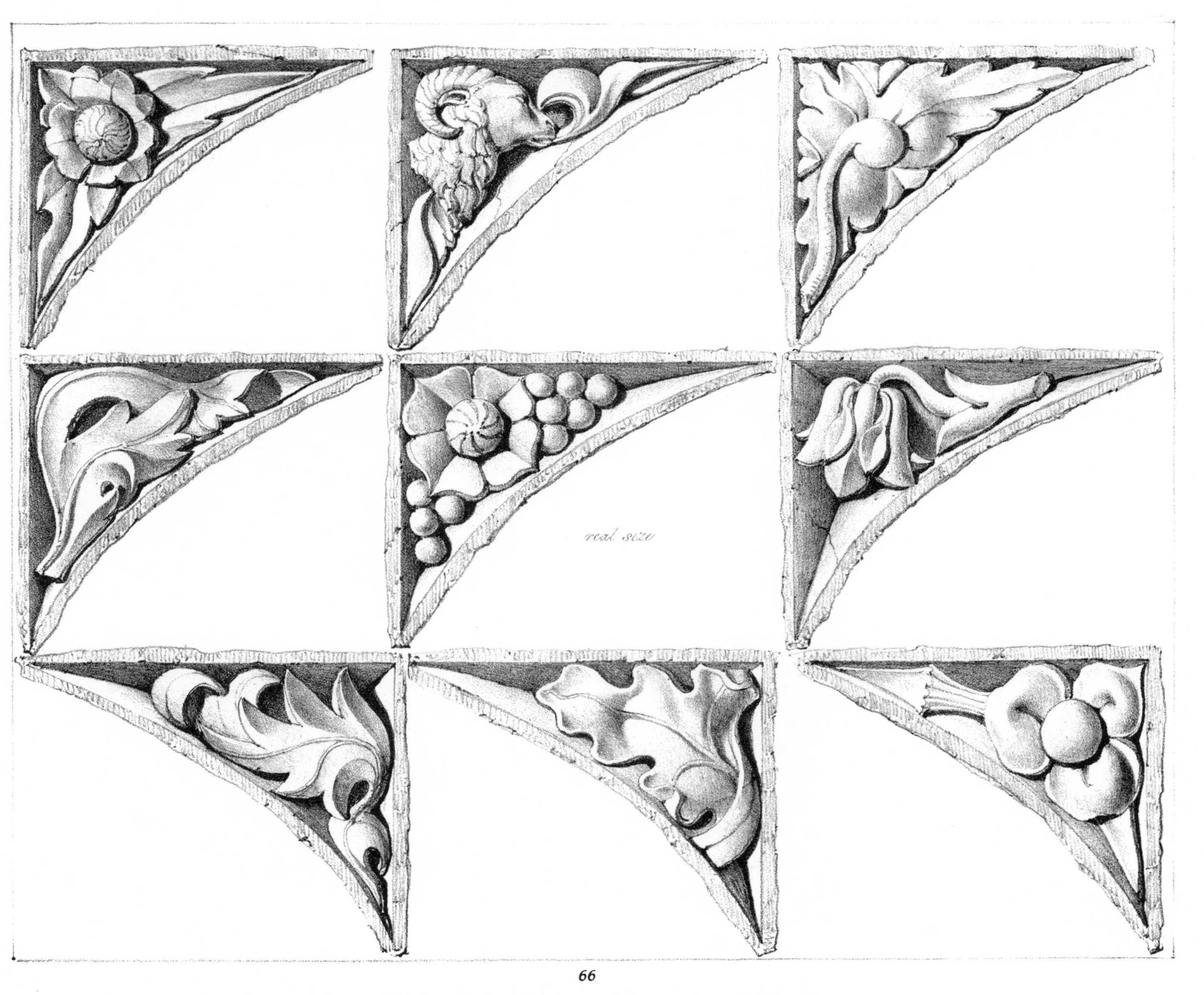

66

Stone spandrels. (Abbot Ramrydge's Chantry, St. Albans Abbey.)

67

Stone ornaments. (St. Albans Abbey. 1: chantry in choir; 2: Duke Humphrey's Chantry.)

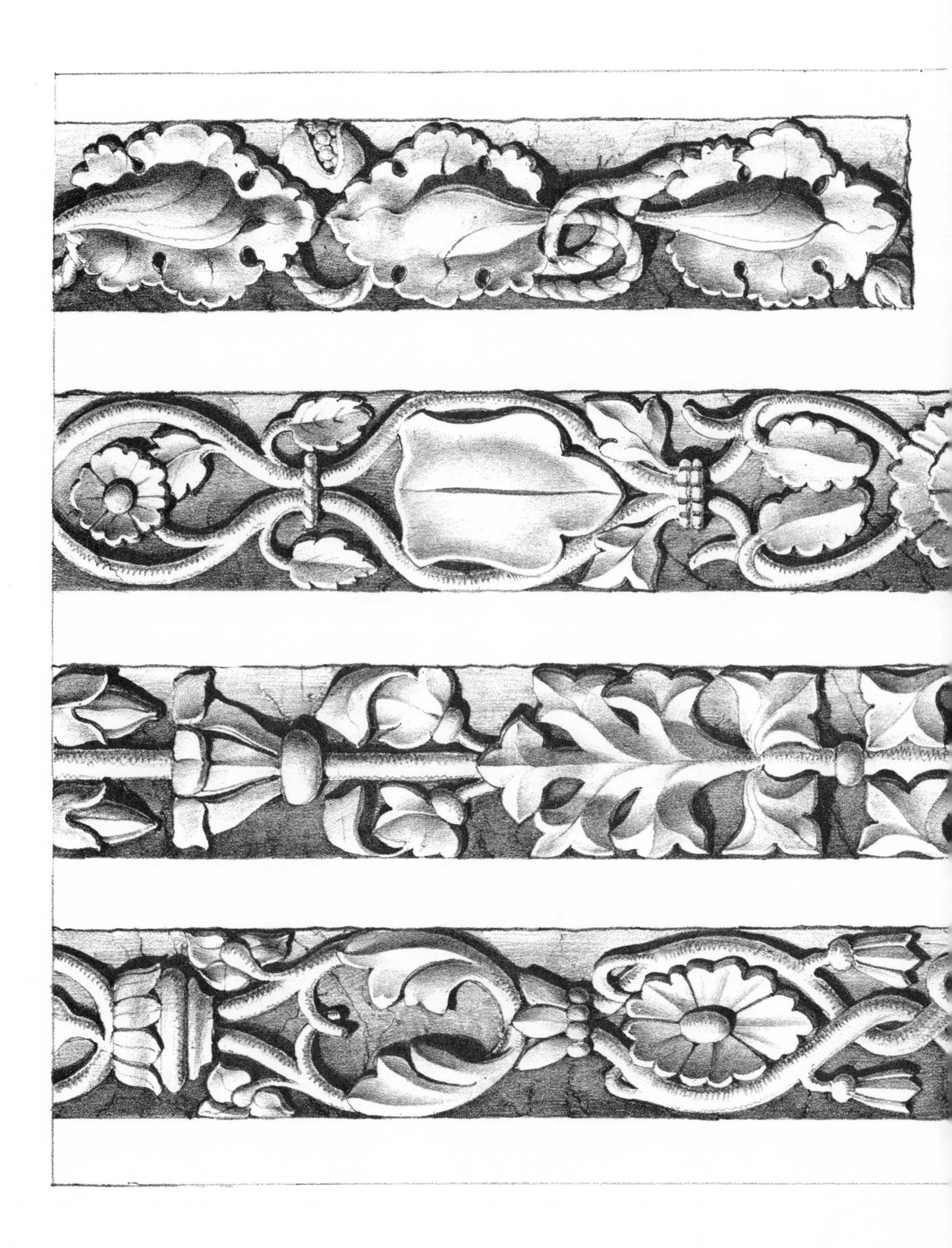

68 & 69

Ornaments. (Chantry of the Countess of Salisbury, Christchurch, Hampshire.)

70

Stone animals. (North entrance, Rouen Cathedral.)

71

Stone paterae. (1–3: Abbot Ramrydge's Chantry, St. Albans Abbey; 4: font, Walsingham Church, Norfolk.)

72

Oak panels. (Beddington Manor House, Surrey.)

73

Wooden stall finials. (New Walsingham Church, Norfolk.)

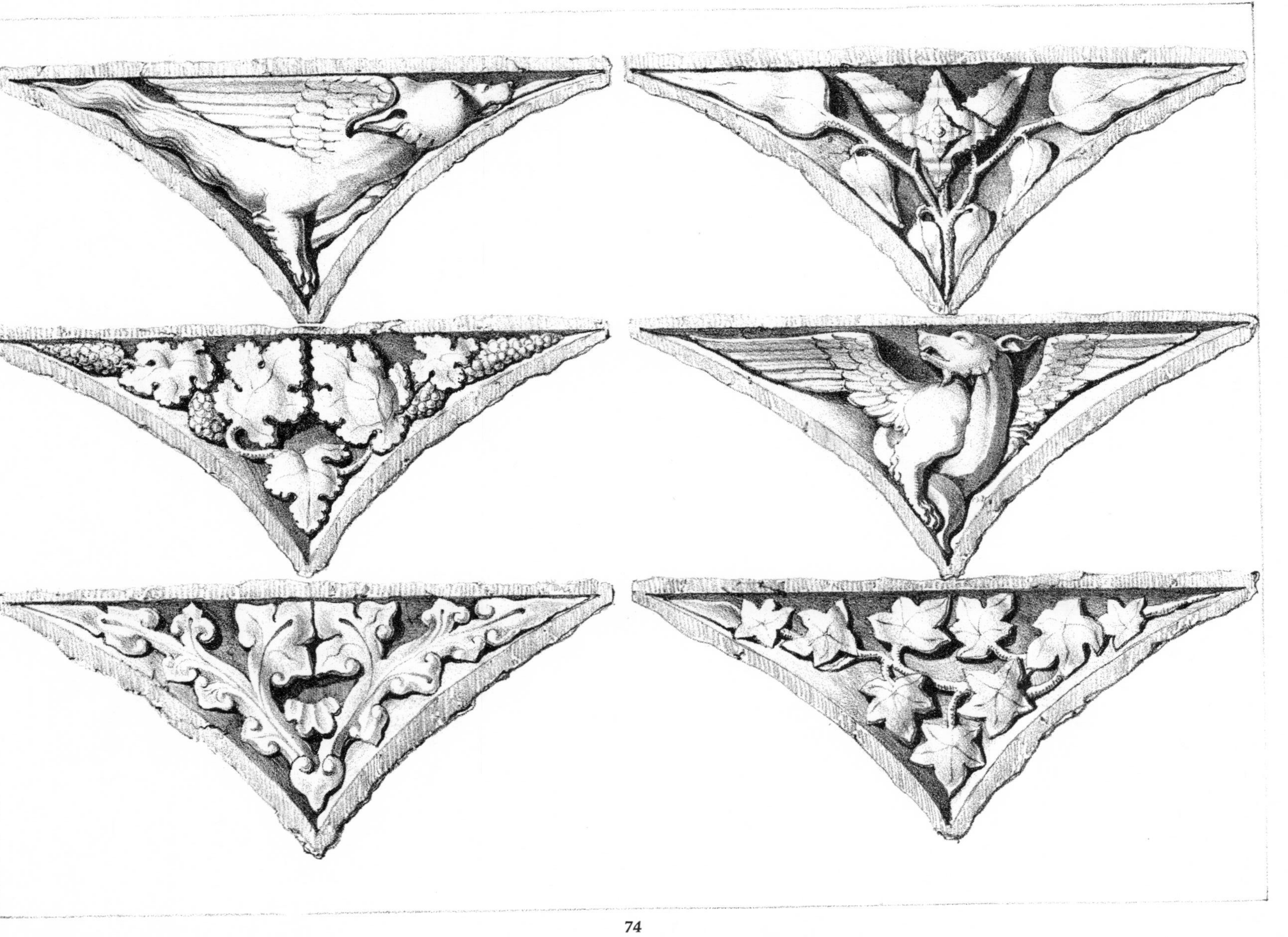

74

Stone spandrels. (Choir, Cathedral of Notre Dame, Paris.)

75

Oak panels. (From a chest, author's collection.)

76

Norman ornaments. (Originally from St. Saviour's Church, Southwark.)

77
Stone capitals between windows. (South aisle, St. Saviour's Church, Southwark.)

78

Stone capitals. (St. Saviour's Church, Southwark.)

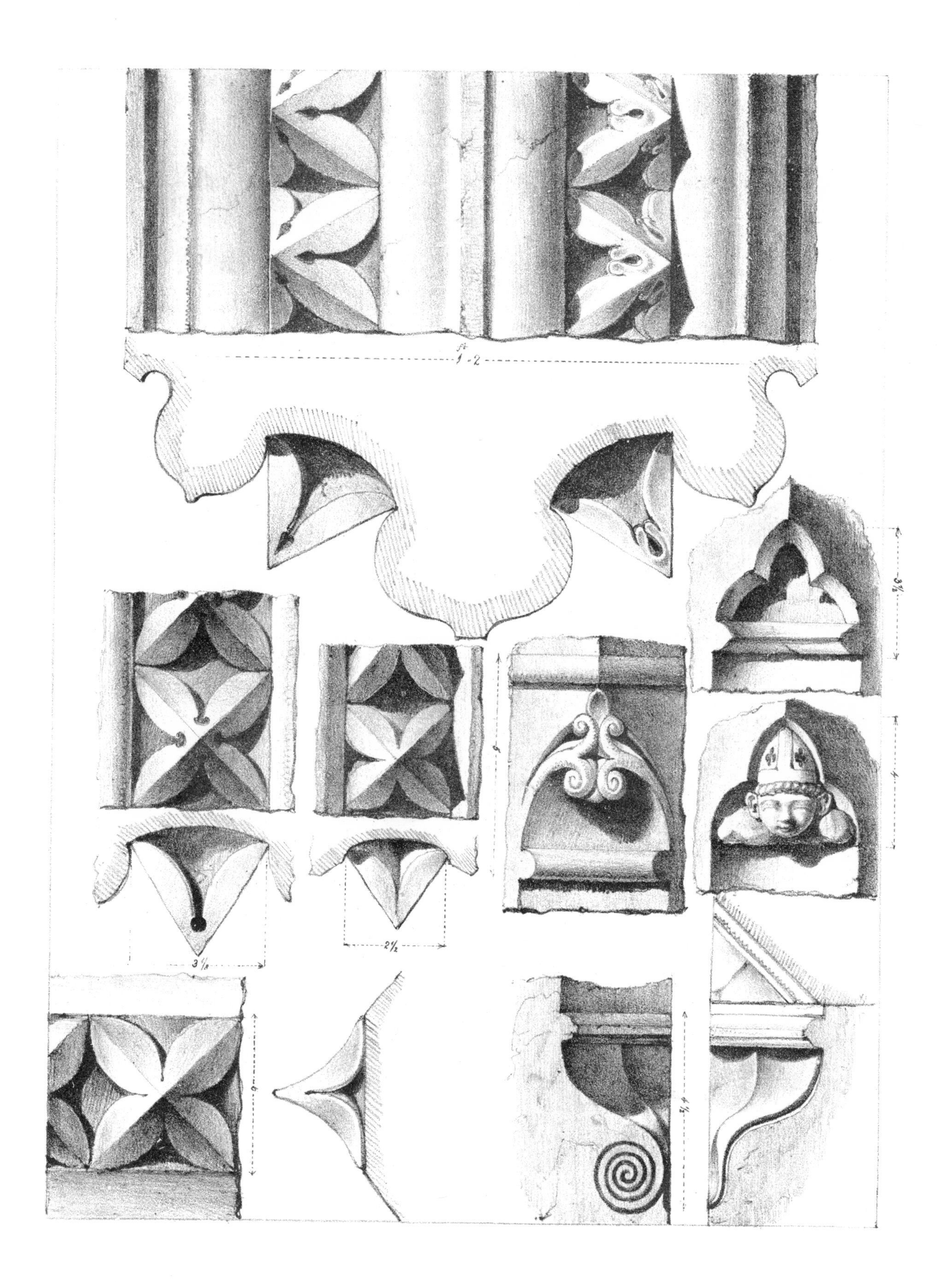

79

Stone ornaments. (St. Saviour's Church, Southwark. 1–4: moldings and dogtooth ornaments; 5–9: ornaments in angle of buttresses.)

80

Stone capitals. (St. George de Boucherville, near Rouen.)

81

Wooden boss. (Collection of J. Adey Repton.)

82

Arms of King Edward the Confessor, impaling the arms of England, as borne by King Henry VI. (Great Hall, Episcopal Palace, Croydon.)

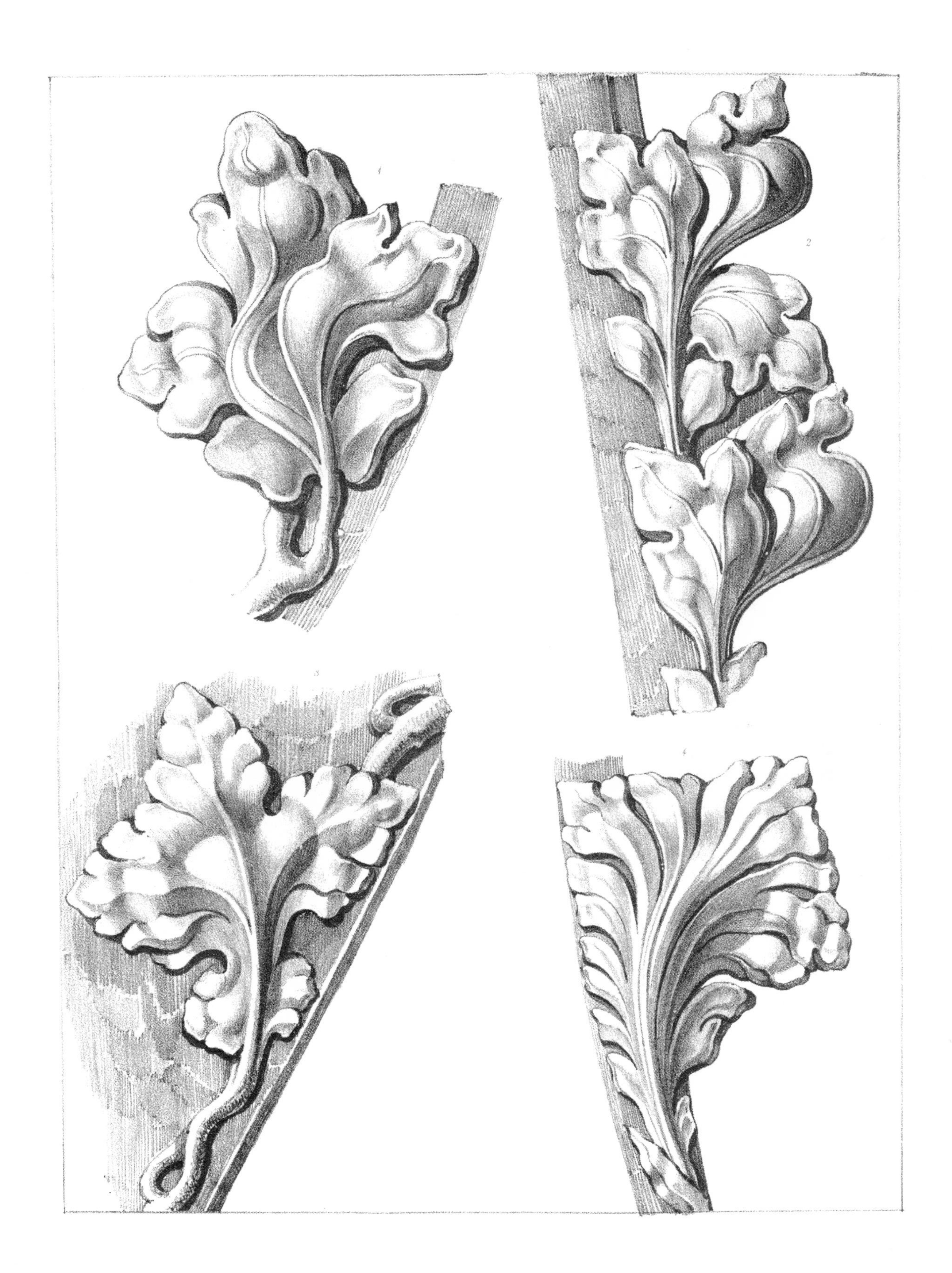

Crockets. (1, 3, 4: stone, York Minster; 2: wood.)

84

Brass figures. (Tomb of Richard Beauchamp, Earl of Warwick, Beauchamp Chapel, St. Mary's Church, Warwick.)

85

Brass figures. (Tomb of Richard Beauchamp, Earl of Warwick, Beauchamp Chapel, St. Mary's Church, Warwick.)

86

Ornaments. (Beauchamp Chapel, St. Mary's Church, Warwick. 1, 2: paterae; 3: stringcourse.)

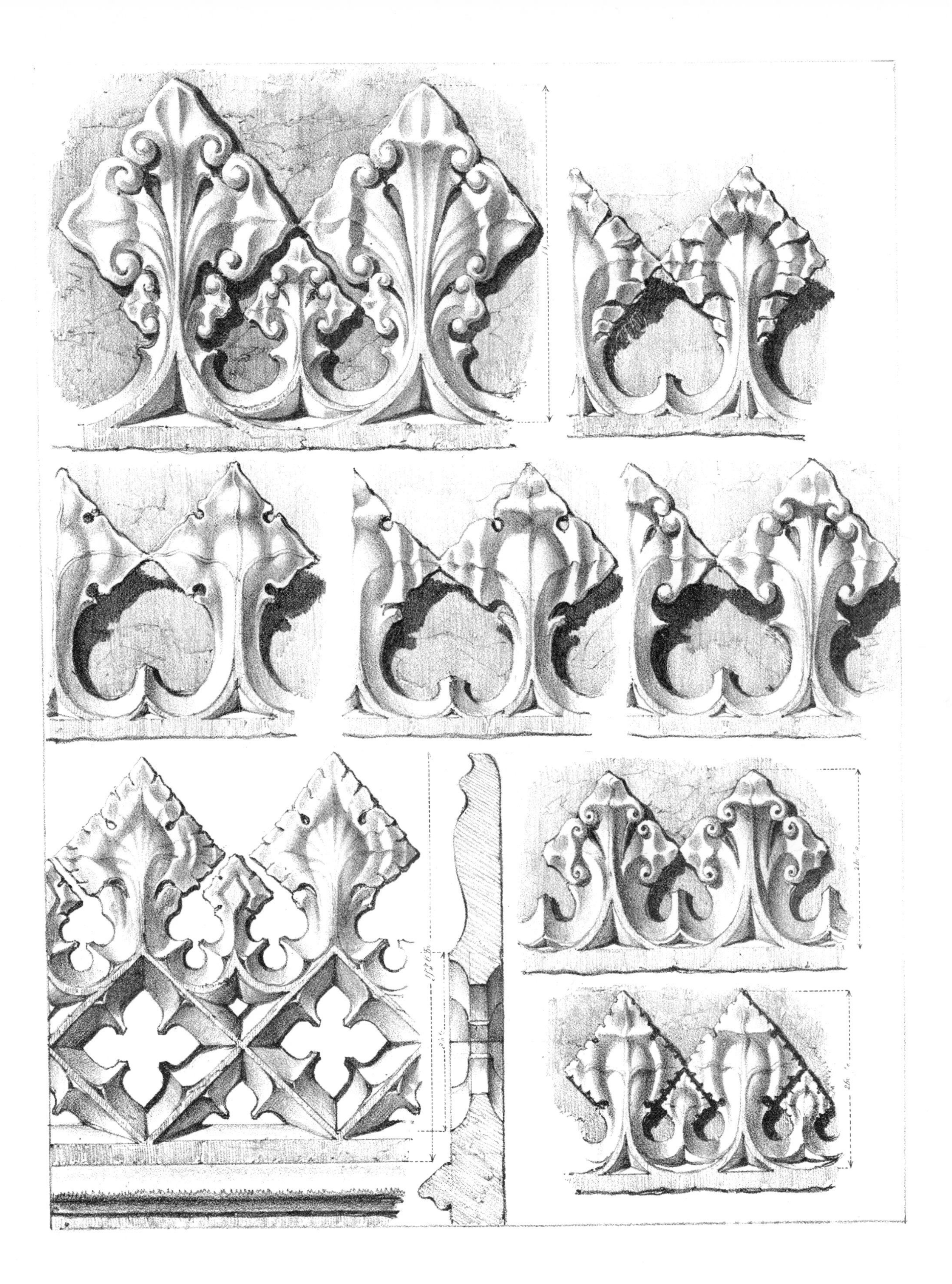

87

Stone strawberry leaves. (Beauchamp Chapel, St. Mary's Church, Warwick; 1: nave, Trinity Church, Stratford-on-Avon.)

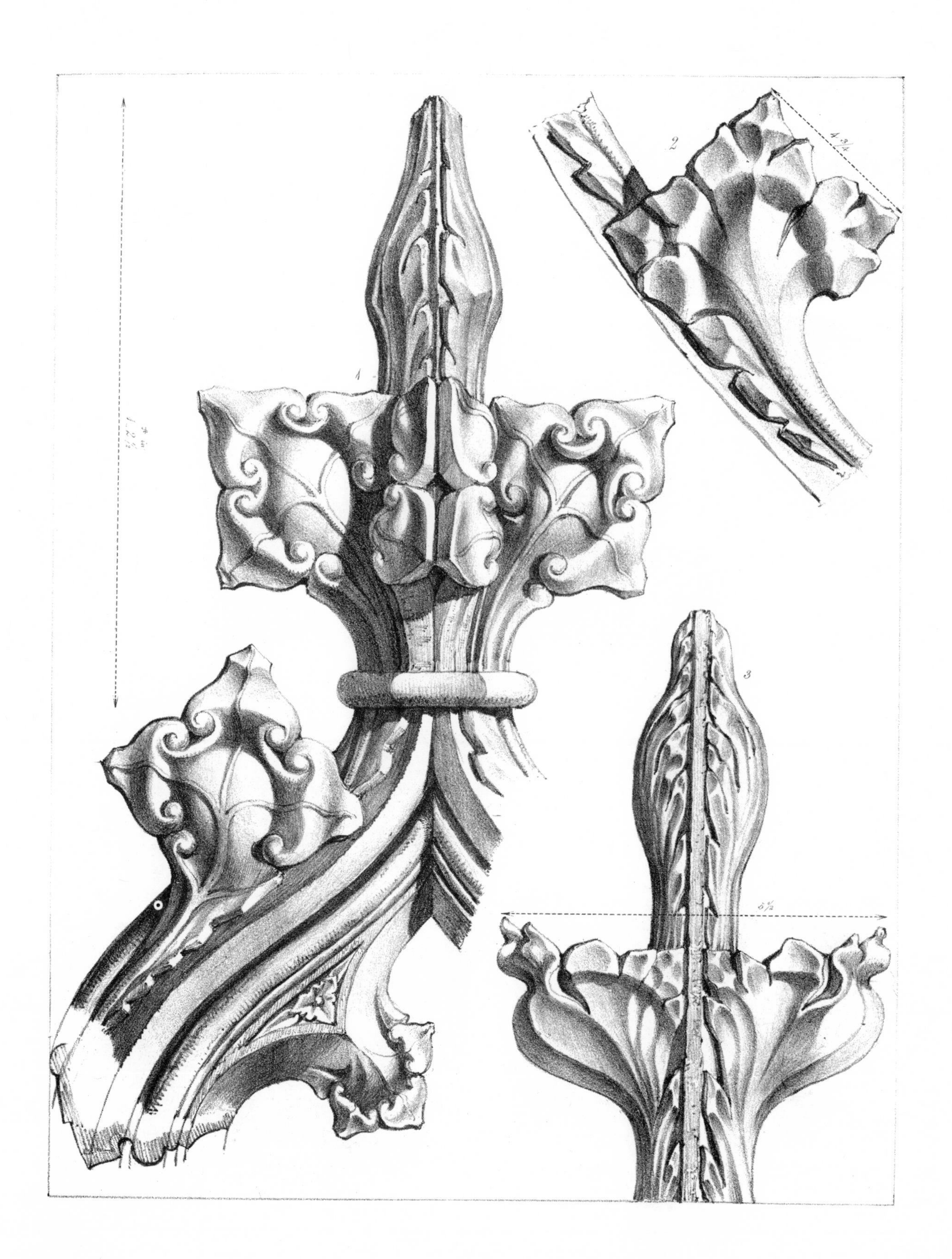

88

Stone finials and crockets. (1, 2: chancel, Trinity Church, Stratford-on-Avon; 3: Beauchamp Chapel, St. Mary's Church, Warwick.)

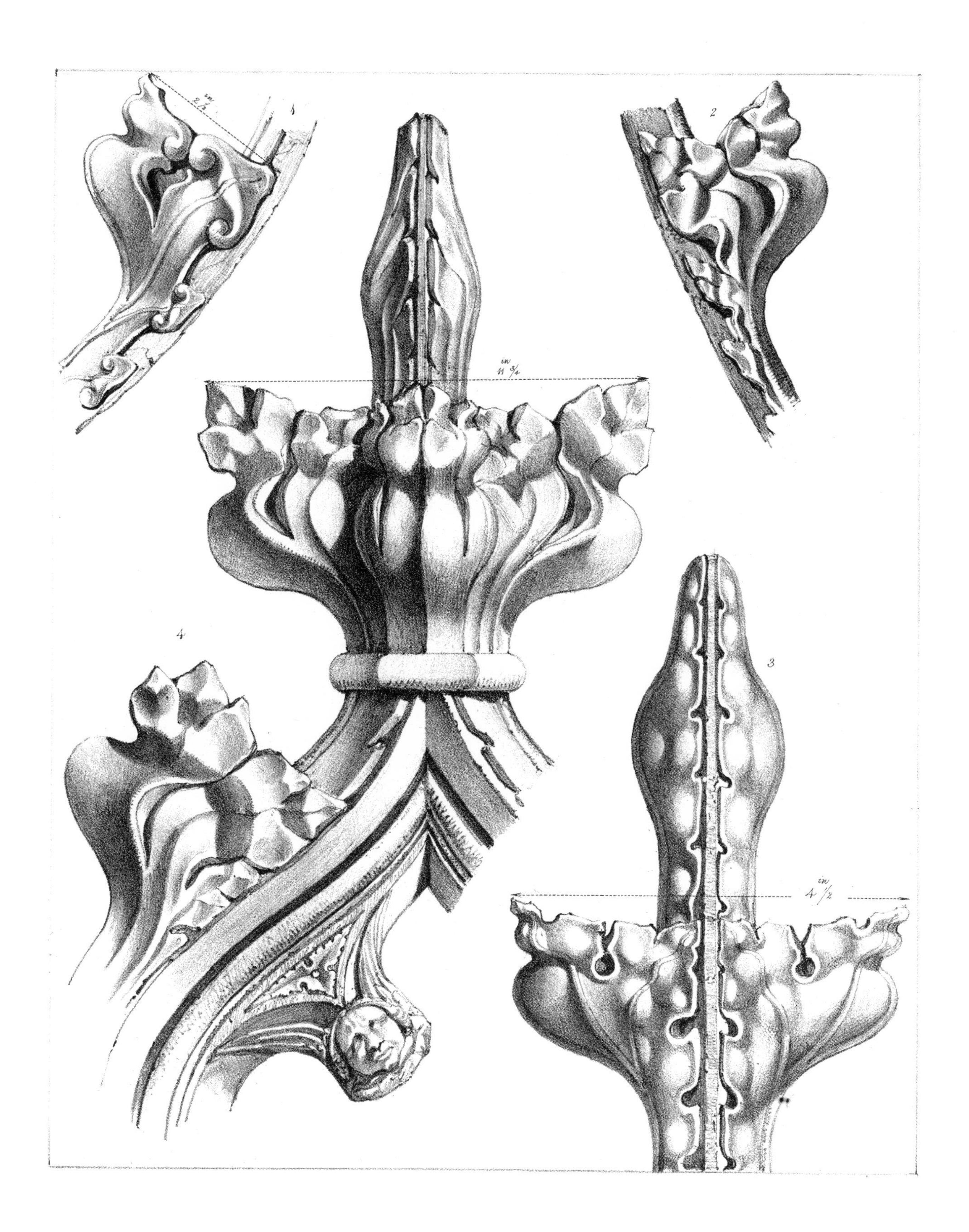

89

Stone ornaments. (1–3: crockets and finial, Beauchamp Chapel, St. Mary's Church, Warwick; 4: finial, Trinity Church, Stratford-on-Avon.)

90

Stone weepers. (Tomb of Richard Beauchamp, Earl of Warwick, St. Mary's Church, Warwick.)

91

Wooden stall finial. (St. Michael's Church, Coventry.)

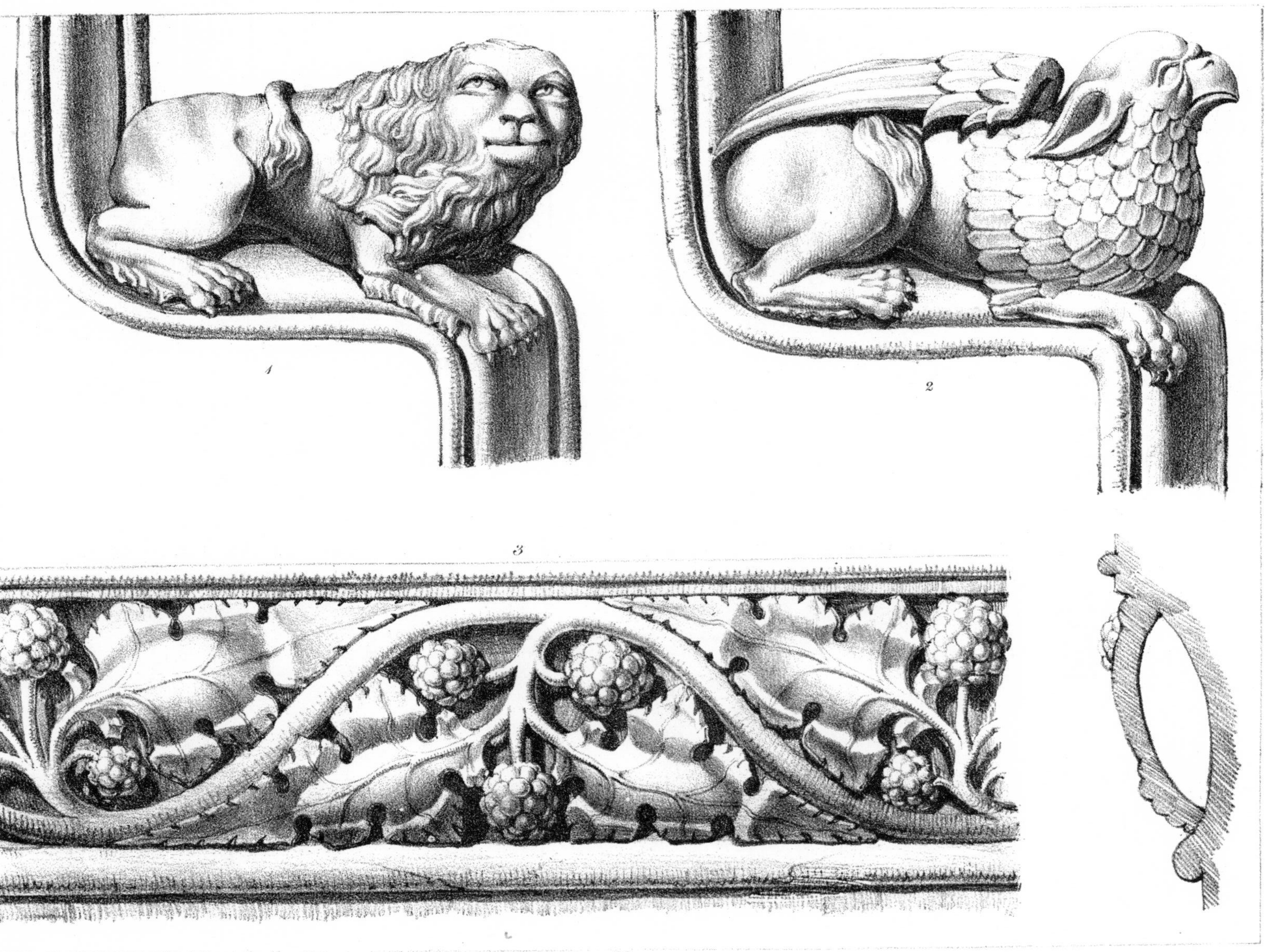

92

Wooden ornaments. (1, 2: stall elbows, Beauchamp Chapel, St. Mary's Church, Warwick; 3: stringcourse, nave, Trinity Church, Stratford-on-Avon.)

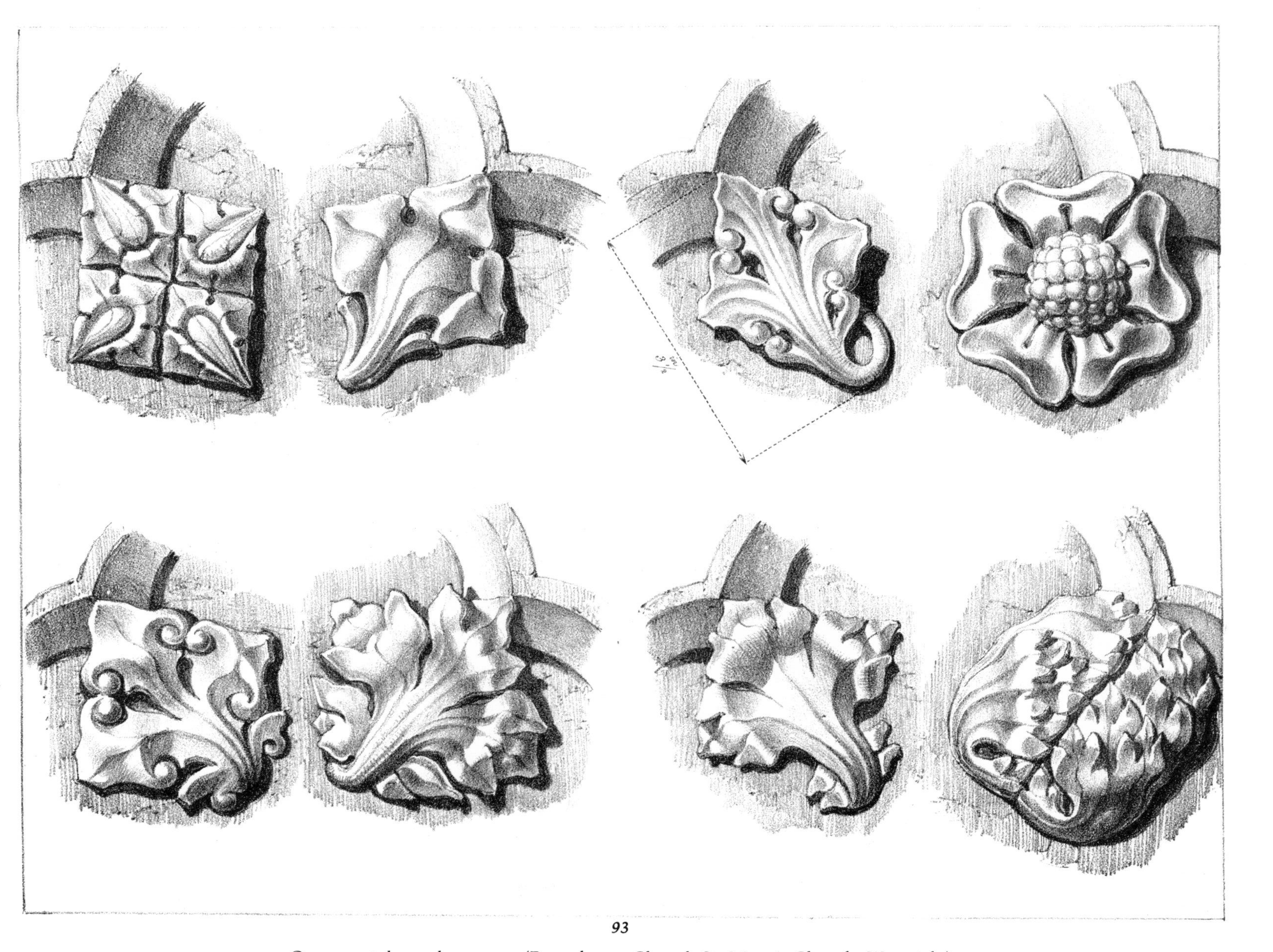

93

Ornamental wooden cusps. (Beauchamp Chapel, St. Mary's Church, Warwick.)

94

Oak tracery. (St. Michael's Church, Coventry.)

95

Oak panels. (Stalls, Henry VII Chapel, Westminster Abbey.)

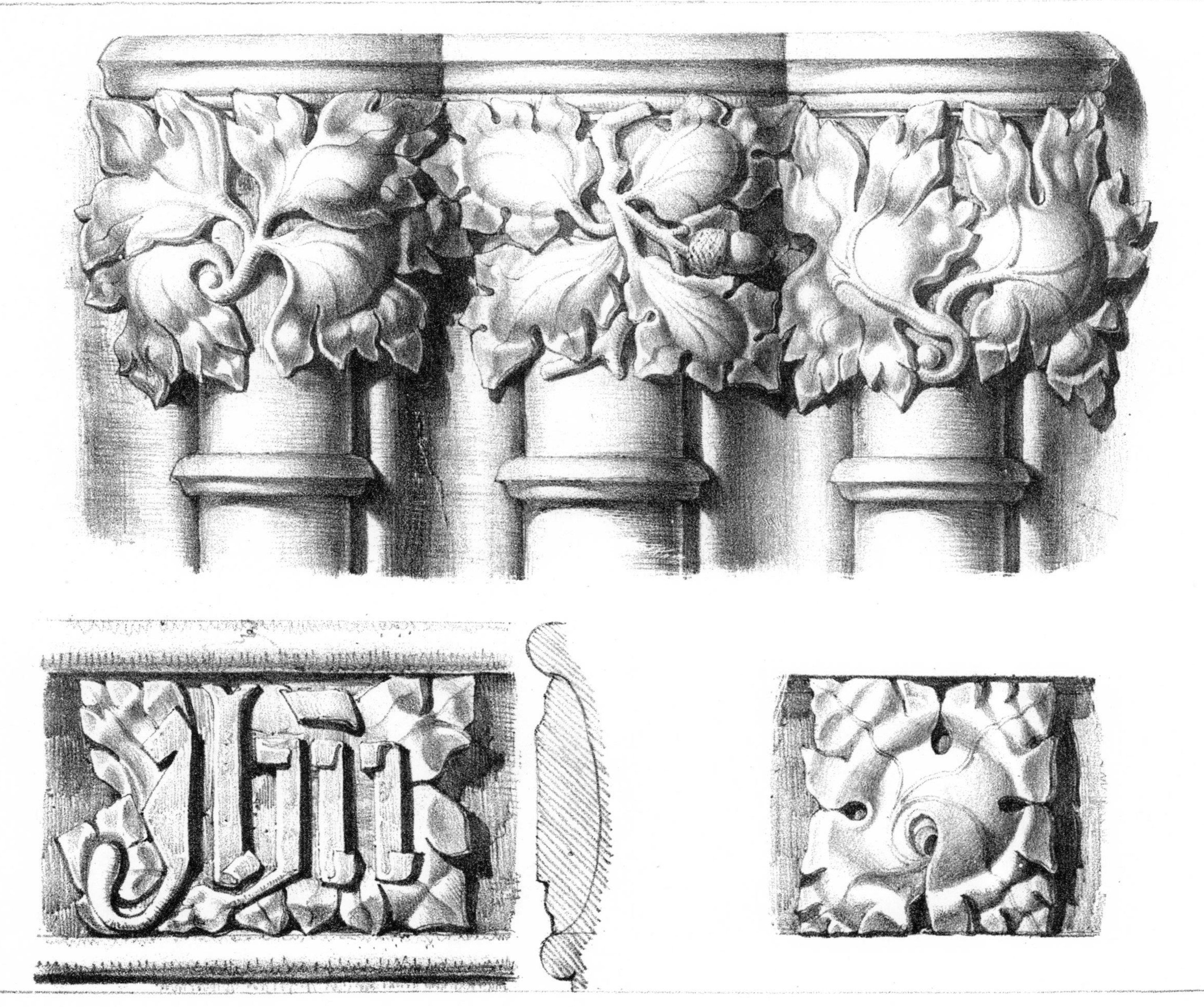

96

Stone ornaments. (1: capitals, entrance to the Great Hall, Kenilworth Castle; 3, 4: paterae, chancel, Trinity Church, Stratford-on-Avon.)

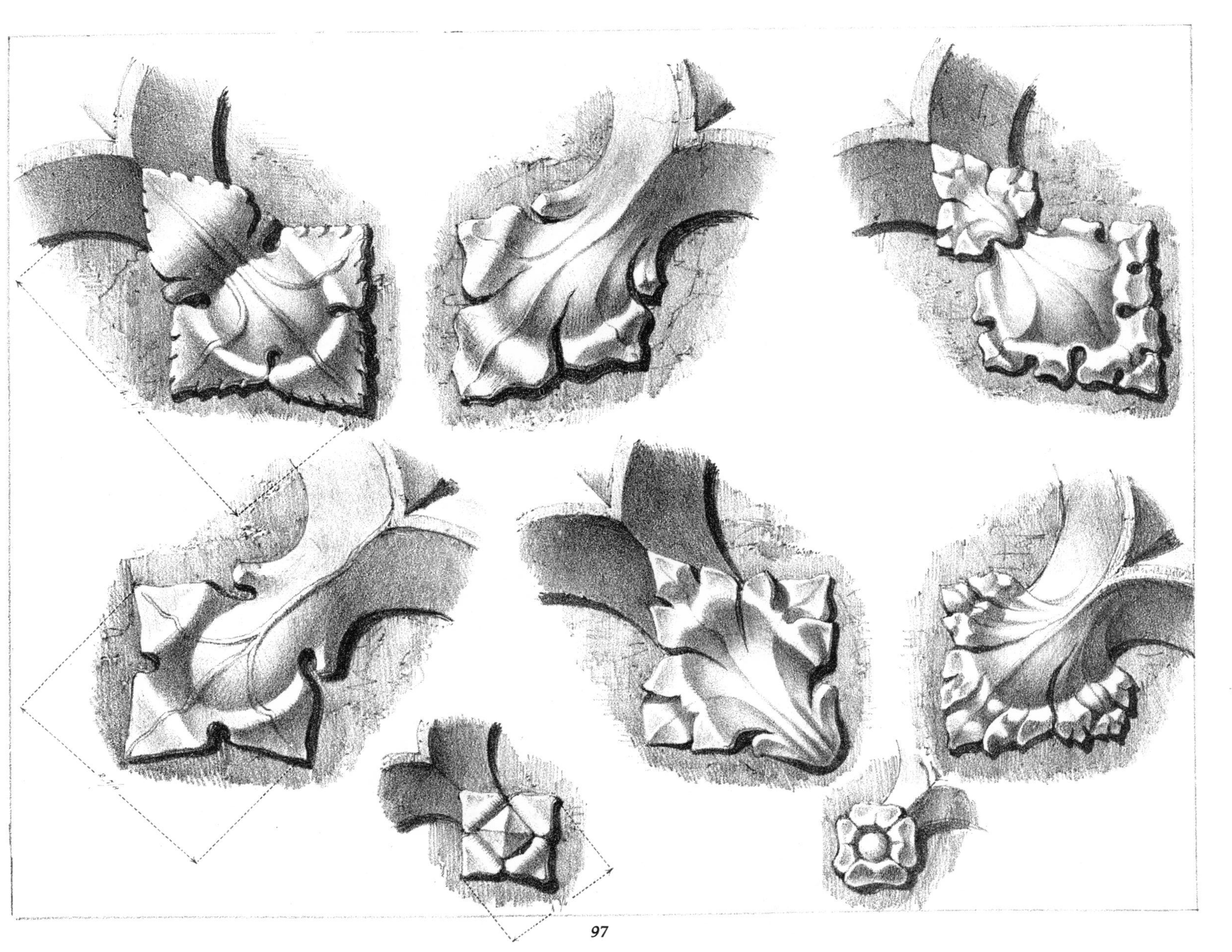

97

Ornamental stone cusps. (Beauchamp Chapel, St. Mary's Church, Warwick.)

98

Stall finials. (Beauchamp Chapel, St. Mary's Church, Warwick.)

99

Stone spandrels. (Beauchamp Chapel, St. Mary's Church, Warwick.)

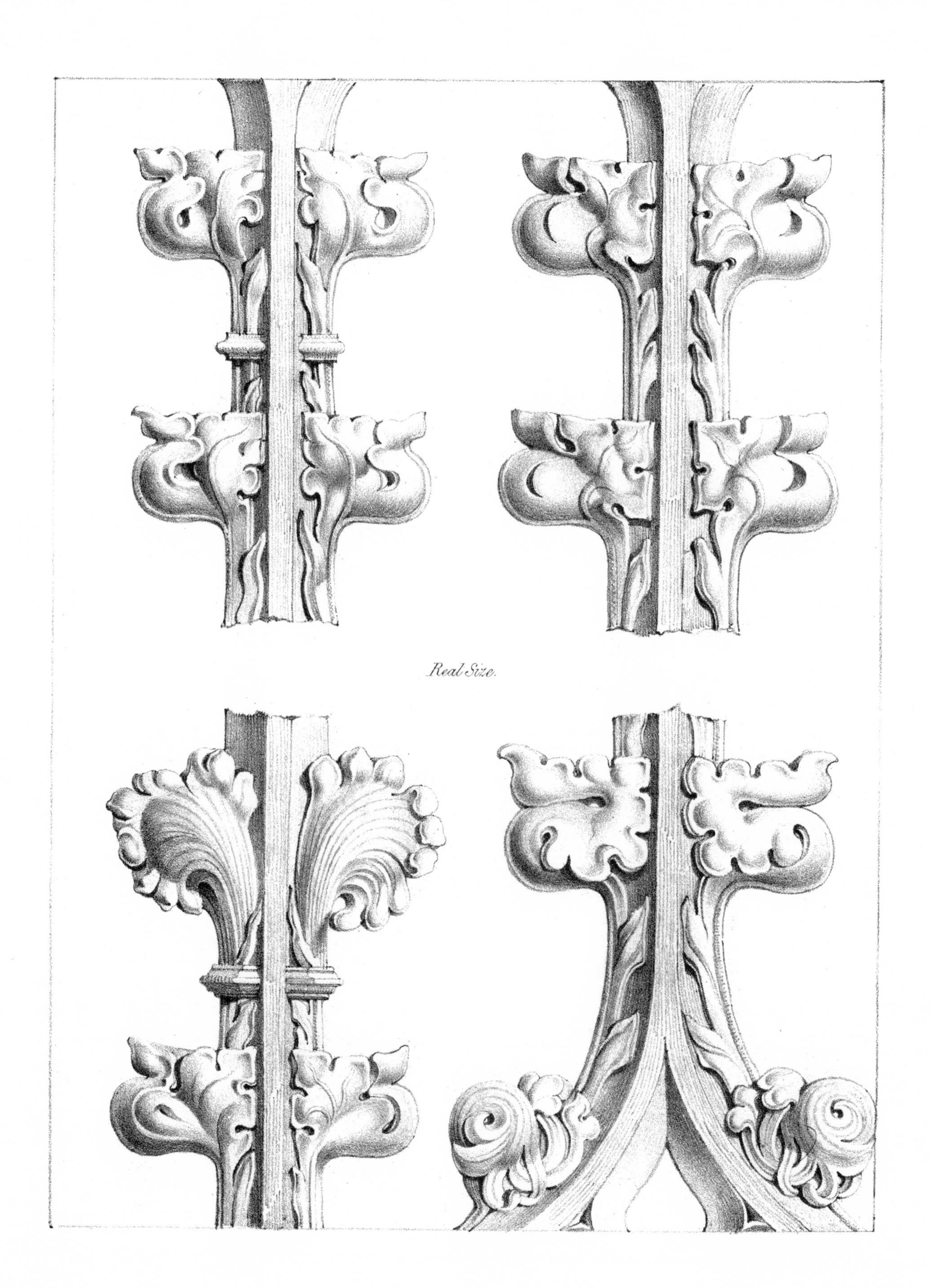

100

Brass crockets. (Shrine, Henry VII Chapel, Westminster Abbey.)